ATHEIST OVERREACH

ATHEIST OVERREACH

What Atheism Can't Deliver

Christian Smith

OXFORD
UNIVERSITY PRESS

OXFORD
UNIVERSITY PRESS

Oxford University Press is a department of the University of Oxford. It furthers
the University's objective of excellence in research, scholarship, and education
by publishing worldwide. Oxford is a registered trade mark of Oxford University
Press in the UK and certain other countries.

Published in the United States of America by Oxford University Press
198 Madison Avenue, New York, NY 10016, United States of America.

Library of Congress Cataloging-in-Publication Data
Names: Smith, Christian, 1960– author.
Title: Atheist overreach : what atheism can't deliver / Christian Smith.
Description: New York, NY : Oxford University Press, [2019] | Includes index.
Identifiers: LCCN 2018009553 | ISBN 9780190880927 (hardcover : alk. paper) |
ISBN 9780190880941 (epub)
Subjects: LCSH: Religion and ethics. | Atheism.
Classification: LCC BJ47.S55 2019 | DDC 211/.8—dc23
LC record available at https://lccn.loc.gov/2018009553

1 3 5 7 9 8 6 4 2

Printed by Sheridan Books, Inc., United States of America

CONTENTS

ATHEIST OVERREACH

Introduction

People the world over today are engaged in big struggles over the viability and importance of religion in personal and public life. Religions throughout human history have been an important feature of most cultures and have been practiced by billions of people. But the modern world has set in motion powerful forces of secularization and, as part of that, recurrent waves of activist atheism have confronted and criticized religion. Most recently in the West, the so-called New Atheism has pressed hard to discredit belief in God and undermine religious influences in society.

In much of Europe, Canada, Australia, and New Zealand, religious beliefs and practices have been declining for decades. The United States, however, appeared for a long time to be an exceptional case to trends of religious decline, seemingly remaining a bastion of religious vitality. Recent evidence suggests, however, that Americans are also starting to abandon religious beliefs and practices.[1] The United States seems to be making a shift toward secularism.[2] The arguments of the New Atheists have been among the influences behind that trend.[3]

Secularism and atheism are not only Western concerns. The forces of secularization and the message of atheism reach around the planet through "carriers" of globalization, such as higher education, the internet, mass consumer capitalism, and liberal politics. At the same time, in many parts of the world, religious leaders and communities of many kinds are pushing back hard against the pressures of secularism; they want nothing to do with what they view as a godless, secular way of life. At stake in this global struggle is the long-term character of human civilizations—whether religions will continue to have a significant place in human life or instead fade into implausibility and social irrelevance.

Central to this contest over religion and secularity are a set of open questions, the answers to which have big consequences for whether religions or secularism have viable long-term futures and how human societies might best be organized. One is *What kind of moral standards are genuinely secular people justified in upholding*? Do secularists have good reasons to be "good without God?" Or, if belief in God fades, will that have moral consequences that most people today would consider harmful? Another important question is *How much can we rely upon the findings of science to know whether or not God exists*? Can science deliver certainty about atheists' claims? Or are the possibilities of human knowledge about God or gods or other possible superhuman forces not subject to scientific answers? A third key question is *Are human beings somehow "naturally" religious*? Does something about natural selection, cognitive wiring in human evolution, or some other factor make religious tendencies an ineradicable feature of human existence? Or could humans as a species actually leave religion behind?

The outcome of today's global struggle over religion and secularity hinges significantly on the answers to these questions. If people can carry on their personal and social lives with functional standards of morality that produce order, happiness, and flourishing, if science really can prove atheism, and if humans can readily leave behind their previously influential religious beliefs and practices, then humanity's long-term future may very well look quite secular. On the other hand if religion actually plays an essential role in upholding desired moral convictions and behaviors, if the findings of science actually do not or cannot endorse atheism, and if it turns out that human beings in fact are "naturally religious" in some important ways, then we should expect religion to persist indefinitely into the future, despite the forces of secularization and atheism.

So, people concerned about matters of religion, secularism, and atheism—whatever position they take—should be very interested in these questions and the best answers to them we can discover. I am. As a sociologist of religion, culture, and morality, I find the ideas and arguments involved in these issues to be fascinating and important. The older I have grown, the less certain about some of the answers I have become. Still, after having thought about these issues long and hard and discussed them with many others, I have come to some definite conclusions. In this book, I offer my best answers to these three crucial questions, in hopes of making a contribution to the ongoing public debate.

This book is different from most books about atheism and religion in that it does not offer an apologetic for either religion or atheism. Nothing in what follows takes a position on whether atheism or any religious claims are correct or not. That is not my concern here. Plenty of other writers have already made such arguments, and none of that has yet resolved the disagreements. I take a different approach to these matters. I do not try to show that atheism as a worldview is fundamentally right or wrong. I focus instead on evaluating certain key positions and claims that many atheists assume or make about science, morality, and human nature. In principle, everything I argue could be correct, and atheism as a general position could still be true. Nonetheless, if even some of what I claim here is right, then at the very least a lot of atheists need to step back and reconsider their positions on some crucial issues. Those positions are not decisive in telling us whether atheism is correct. But they do matter a great deal for how atheism advances its cause, the kind of claims atheists can make with intellectual honesty, and the sort of new world that atheism can expect to bring into being if as a movement it succeeds.

My overarching argument in this book is captured by its title. Atheism, in many of its current expressions, I maintain, is *overreaching*. Many contemporary atheist activists are trying to claim too much, attempting to establish positions that are unwarranted, going overboard in confidence and enthusiasm in prosecuting their positions. Again, that does not in and of itself say that atheists are right or wrong. I merely contend that—whatever the truth status of atheism—many of its current advocates are overextending themselves in certain important assumptions, arguments, and conclusions. For atheists, who claim to be advocates of stern reason, realism, and intellectual honesty, that is a big problem, a "performative contradiction." To live up to their own standards, if I am correct, these atheists will need to pull back from their overreaching. And doing so will have significant implications for the larger, global struggle over religion and secularism.

Rather than weighing in on one side or another of this debate, I want in this book to help the argument move forward in a more intellectually clear, honest, and fair way. It seems to me that if the religion-versus-secularism struggle is going to proceed in an open and fruitful a manner, all parties will need to be carefully heard, appraised, and, where necessary, criticized. I attempt that here on certain issues important to atheism. I do not pretend to accomplish it comprehensively. No single book could do that. My contribution is more modest.

How so? For one thing, this book scrutinizes only the atheist side of the debate. A similar critical exercise could also well be conducted on some religious apologists, as indeed more than a few atheist critics have already done. This book also only engages the atheist authors most relevant to the concerns I raise. Not many of my arguments engage the most famous of the New Atheists— Richard Dawkins, Christopher Hitchens, Daniel Dennett, and Sam Harris, who tend to attract most of the attention and controversy. Instead I take on a broader swath of somewhat lesser known atheist writers.[4] I think it enhances the debate to look beyond "the usual suspects." Furthermore, I address only a limited set of concerns— namely, the three key questions about morality, science, and human religiousness—setting aside a host of other potentially relevant questions and criticisms. I have no interest in marshaling an ency- clopedic critique of atheism. I focus instead on what strike me as crucial weak spots in the arguments of many atheists today.

This book can be read as a collection of essays rather than a single, progressively unfolding argument, meaning that each chapter can be read on its own and in any order, depending on one's interest.[5] Altogether, however, they emphasize the same overarching theme of atheists' *overreach*. The four chapters of this book proceed as follows. The first engages the important question of whether human beings have good reason to be morally "good without God," as most atheists today claim we do. In that exploration I engage the works of a broad sample of contemporary atheist moralists who insist that we humans not only *can* be but also have *good reasons* to be morally upright without God. I argue that the atheist moralists I examine are not so much flat wrong as simply grossly overreaching in their claims. I conclude that, in all intellectual honesty, people inhabiting an atheist universe do seem to have good reasons to be moderately "good," to behave morally in a provisional and limited sense; but they do not have good reasons to live up to the high standards of moral goodness demanded by the inclusive, universal humanism that many atheist moralists advocate.

The second chapter follows on the same theme by taking a different angle on a related question. It examines in more expansive terms the question whether people inhabiting a naturalistic universe (that is, one in which only the energy and matter of nature exist, nothing supernatural) are reasonably justified in demanding moral commitments to the kind of universal benevolence and human rights that most atheists, as well as religious believers, today wish to champion and defend. I argue that naturalism does not seem to justify such demands. Naturalism may well justify many important substantive moral responsibilities but not, as far as I can see, a commitment to honor universal benevolence and human rights.

The third chapter shifts focus to the question of what the findings of modern science can and cannot tell us about the existence of God. Here we deal not with ethics (the focus of the first two chapters) but instead with epistemology—that is, what we humans can properly know. Many contemporary atheist writers claim that the findings of science establish the fact that God does not exist. This chapter contests that claim, showing that—whether God exists or not—no such conclusion can be properly drawn from the discoveries of science. I offer some crucial distinctions that I hope help to clarify the much-debated and often misunderstood relationship between science and religion.

The fourth and final chapter shifts the focus to the question of whether or not human beings are in any significant way "naturally religious," as some religious apologists say. The relevance of this question is clear. If this claim is erroneous and is perhaps a mere self-serving ideology, then the activist atheist agenda for the future faces much better chances of success. If religion in human minds and societies is not grounded in stubborn human nature, it is instead a mere contingency or dispensable phase of human history. If on the other hand humans possess some natural tendencies to be religious, then the (at least militant) atheist goal of ridding the world of religion faces a serious uphill battle and may be doomed to failure. I suggest in this chapter that humans are indeed naturally religious, when the meaning of "naturally" is correctly specified, but as a matter of natural capacities and tendencies, not in any deterministic way. I then spell out for atheism the implications of such an understanding of natural human religiousness.

I attempt in this book to avoid a strident, partisan tone, even if at times I am polemical to make a point. My purpose here, again, is not to help one side or another of this larger debate to "win". I seek instead to engage the debate differently, proceeding in the tentative faith that, through the clash of strong rival arguments and replies, weak arguments will falter in the end and good arguments will prevail. To encourage that kind of intellectual advance—gained through agonistic conflict among rival claimants—this book seeks to sharpen the intellectual clarity, honesty, and precision of the arguments and claims in the ongoing debate itself. I hope that, in the larger process, my criticisms will help lead to greater insight and perhaps, dare I say, enlightenment.

Finally, a word about my intended audience. I do not advance my arguments here as an original contribution to the detailed and more sophisticated debates of professional philosophers in the fields of philosophy of religion, ethics, science, and human rights. My explorations are too basic and incomplete for that audience. I do hope philosophers read this book, and I have included scholarly notes that speak to some of their concerns. But I also intend this book to be an accessible invitation to the educated reading public and to undergraduate college students to join or to continue participating in well-informed conversations about the relative merits of religious and nonreligious conceptions of morality, science, and humanity. The question of atheist overreach involves matters too broadly important to be left only to professional philosophers to analyze in scholarly publications. We must take seriously the best of what philosophers argue.[6] But many nonprofessionals often need on-ramps to access and begin to get up to speed on issues addressed in more complex and specialized academic debates. I intend this book as one such on-ramp.

Chapter 1

Just How "Good without God" Are Atheists Justified in Being?

Suppose that tomorrow everyone on earth woke up and decided that no God, gods, or superhuman powers or forces existed. Everyone became an atheist. What kind of moral commitments would humanity then rationally be justified affirming, promoting, and living?

This chapter examines the question—much debated of late—of whether humans can be "good without God." I focus on arguments advanced by activist atheists who answer this question in the affirmative, claiming that a robust, universal, humanistic ethic of care and respect for the rights and well-being of all other human beings can be derived rationally from atheism. I evaluate these arguments by conducting a close reading of a body of texts addressing the matter. To preview, I will argue the following.

First, *of course* atheists *can* be good despite not believing in God. I witness this empirical fact around me and suspect that most everyone else does too. When asked if he believed in infant baptism, Mark Twain once replied, "Believe in it? Hell, I've seen it!" On the simple empirical question of whether atheists *can* be good, my answer is the same.[1]

However, we need to distinguish between the practical fact of many atheists' evident capacity for "being good" and the philosophical question of what kinds of goodness atheism actually rationally warrants. Just because someone *can* and *does* act "good" does not mean they necessarily have good reasons to do so.[2] And if they do not have compelling reasons, perhaps they or their children will eventually wise up and stop acting so good.

Third, I will say that we need to disaggregate monolithic and ill-defined notions of what "good" is—that is, what we mean when using the adjective "good"—by identifying and describing distinct versions of what "being good" might entail. Most arguments in this debate proceed by assuming an implicit good-bad binary, as if people's lives are either simply "good" or "bad," which is crude and obfuscating. We need to work out more helpful distinctions to make better sense of the issues. I will distinguish what I will call "modest" or "moderate" expectations of goodness that are fairly demanding from "high" or "strong" expectations that are universalistic and very demanding.

I will conclude that atheists are rationally justified in living according to a certain conception of moral standards that we can rightly call "good," but that this standard ought to be ethically modest, setting no more than a moderately high bar of moral expectations on human behavior. And this modest standard of morality falls far short of the kind of robust, universal, humanistic morality that most atheist activists have in mind today when they insist that we can be "good without God."

I went into this inquiry with a genuinely open mind, interested to see if atheists really could make a solid case for the rational justification for a strong morality. I read nearly all the relevant recent works directed at (mostly) popular audiences that I could get my hands on, written both by scholars and atheist activists (my intention is to engage more accessible works designed to influence mainstream culture, rather than to drill down into the technical literature on the topic in academic philosophy journals). My analysis here focuses on a close reading of four particular works. They are Philip Kitcher, *Life after Faith* (along with Kitcher's more in-depth companion book *The Ethical Project*); Sam Harris, *The Moral Landscape*; Greg Epstein, *Good without God*; and Lex Bayer and John Figdor, *Atheist Mind, Humanist Heart*.[3] These books' authors include two academic scholars (Kitcher is a philosopher and Harris a neuroscientist), two humanist chaplains at Ivy League universities (Epstein and Figdor), and a leader of an atheist nonprofit (Bayer). In addition, I read and will sometimes refer to related works, such as Frans de Waal, *The Bonobo and the Atheist*; Phil Zuckerman, *Living the Secular Life*, Katherine Ozment, *Grace without God*, Walter Sinnott-Armstrong, *Morality without God?*, Kai Nielsen, *Ethics without God*, and Ronald Lindsay, *The Necessity of Secularism*.[4] These books offer a representative sampling of what today are presented in popular culture as the best arguments for being "good without God." I will refer to the authors as "atheist moralists."

Two last preliminary points. First, this chapter should not be construed as a positive defense of religion or religious ethics. That is not my purpose. I am concerned here only with evaluating the recent atheists' claim that humanity can be "good without God." I do not here take on any burden of offering a constructive alternative to atheist ethics.

Second, this chapter emphasizes the idea of having good reasons for moral behavior. I must clarify why I think that matters. I do not think that good reasons directly determine people's moral actions. Humans are not simple rationalists who follow the best ideas. People's behavior is influenced by many, often conflicting reasons, forces, and emotions. Other influences can override the genuinely good reasons people have to act a certain way. However, having good reasons for moral commitments still matters, for at least three reasons. First, even if having a good reason for it does not *guarantee* moral behavior, most people are more likely to behave in ways for which they believe they have good reasons than in ways for which they lack them. Unjustified cultural norms can propel costly behaviors, but not indefinitely; eventually people begin to question them and, lacking a good justification, may adjust the moral norms. Second, when good reasons are culturally shared, they often become *institutionalized*. At issue here is not merely isolated moral actors, but institutional practices, expectations, and habits that shape behaviors long-term and contextually. Over the long run, institutionalized cultural and moral norms rarely rise above the best ideas and reasons that leaders can articulate and people can believe. If we want good institutions that last, we need good reasons explaining them. Third, rationality and intellectual honesty require that we evaluate important claims; and if we cannot find good reasons to justify them, then on philosophical grounds the claims must be judged lacking.

But what are "good reasons?" When it comes to justifying potentially costly moral behaviors for real human beings as we actually are, to have good reasons requires two parts: a warranting explanation and a justifying motivation. The first aspect of having a good reason for moral action is understanding the rationale for such action (the warranting explanation). The second aspect is understanding why one actually *should care* about the elements of the explanation (the motivation) enough to act upon it, especially when it is costly. It is possible to possess a logical explanation for "being good" that lacks a sufficient motivating justification to care about and act upon it (just as it is possible to be *motivated* to "be good" when one actually has no rational explanatory warrant for doing so).[5] By my account, then, a good reason for being "good without God" must entail *both* an explanation and a motivation for why people should be so. On this point I part ways with rationalist Kantian ethics, which insists that warranting explanations always contain their own justifying motivations, so that all any person needs is a reasoned account for why an action is right or wrong, and that ought automatically to motivate any rational person to conform to her duty of obeying the moral law. I believe Kantians are misguided, and I maintain that a truly good reason for moral actions requires both a warranting explanation and a motivational justification.[6]

HOW GOOD WITHOUT GOD OUGHT WE TO BE?

So, what kind of morally good living[7] do our moralists say atheism can generate and sustain, and how and why so? None of these authors are highly systematic or clear about exactly what "good" is. A few are muddled and unclear. Sometimes they describe moral goodness with vague phrases like "behaving ethically," our "deepest values," and helping others to "be more of a person."[8] But let us concentrate on the clearest of what they write.

These atheist moralists begin their arguments by setting a fairly low bar for human goodness, focusing first on the kind of basic transactional behaviors that sociobiologists and evolutionary psychologists emphasize—namely, cooperation, reciprocity, fairness, restraint on aggression, kin altruism, conflict reduction, and earned reputations of trustworthiness.[9] Those basic goods are not very morally demanding. So the claims escalate.

Atheism, we continue to read, justifies much stronger moral goods. These include kindness, compassion, refraining from hurting others, respecting and providing aid for others, solidarity, taking responsibility, commitment to the truth, "prosocial feeling," and concern for the common good.[10] These are not simply ways to make self-interested social exchanges more efficient and pleasant. They demand genuinely caring about at least some other people and expending oneself for them. In fact, many of these authors say that their ethical approach can be summarized by the Golden Rule: "Do unto others as you would have them do unto you."[11]

These atheist moralists, however, do not settle for these arguably more realistic ethical aspirations and obligations. They push up the moral stakes to more elevated heights, calling for an egalitarian and universalistic humanism that requires honoring the dignity and rights of all human persons everywhere. According to Philip Kitcher, for example, atheism justifies a morality that compels everyone to work toward "remedying or ameliorating the plight of millions, even billions," in order to provide all humans with "the opportunity for a worthwhile life."[12] Atheism, he says, compels us to become "responsive to the desires of the entire human population" and so to afford the "provision of equal opportunities for worthwhile lives for all" and the redistribution of "basic resources for the poor" so that "the necessities of life can be stably maintained for all." These, he writes, must include "quality education and medical care . . . distributed to all" in order to realize social equality. This is not mere social cooperation. It sets a very high moral standard indeed, requiring real sacrifice by the haves for the benefit of the have-nots.

Greg Epstein says that atheism justifies our leading "ethical lives of personal fulfillment that aspire to the greater good of humanity," "treating each person as having an inherent worth and dignity" and "improving society . . . and developing global community." This will require that we "minimize inequalities of circumstances . . . and . . . support a just distribution of natural resources"; honor diversity, respect, human rights, civil liberties, open participation in the democratic process; and fulfill a "planetary duty to protect nature's integrity, diversity, and beauty in a secure, sustainable manner." Everyone, he says, will have to learn to practice "voluntary simplicity" and to promote global sustainability requiring the constraint of consumption.[13]

Sam Harris, for his part, says that being good without God involves promoting "happiness for the greatest number of people" and "maximiz[ing] personal and collective well-being" for all of humanity.[14] And Beyer and Figdor write that atheism obliges people to create "the greatest life-happiness for [other] people in society."[15] In short, our contemporary atheist moralists assure us that we humans still can and must aspire to a highly demanding version of a universalistic, egalitarian, and inclusive humanism.[16]

WHY BE GOOD WITHOUT GOD?

What kind of moral reasoning in the absence of the divine could give rise to such lofty moral commitments? Each author spells out a somewhat different rationale for being so very good without God. All of their arguments, however, rely on a combination of pragmatic functionalism, enlightened self-interest, and social-contract reasoning. "Pragmatic functionalism" here means appealing to the predictable practical results that certain human norms and behaviors tend to generate in real life, focusing on how things actually tend to work when people interact in different ways (for example, with trust and cooperation instead of suspicion and hostility).[17] Arguments appeal to enlightened self-interest when they observe that people are generally able to gain greater rewards in the long run by behaving nicely than by behaving selfishly. Social-contract reasoning suggests that people do or should agree to establish and enforce shared norms of behavior that, if upheld, will improve their collective well-being. These authors supplement these reasons with various appeals to Adam Smith's writings about natural human moral "sentiments," Kantian rational universalizing,[18] Benthamite utilitarianism, the reproductive-fitness value of kinship selection and reciprocal altruism, and explorations of game-theory experiments, such as the prisoner's dilemma and the philosopher's so-called trolley problem.

Sam Harris's argument for being good is simple. All humans at all times and everywhere, he says, want to enjoy lives free from suffering, anxiety, and want. All people desire health, safety, security, pleasure, and prosperity. We all want to live good lives that go well. The one universal human motivation, in short, is to maximize our well-being. We can also learn through experience and, increasingly, science how to improve human life. And one thing we learn, he says, is that life is vastly improved when people practice moral goods, such as reciprocity, kindness, respect, fairness, self-restraint, and compassion for others. Therefore, it is in our individual and collective self-interest to be good to each other. No religious rationale is needed—only pragmatic social learning, enlightened self-interest, and rational social agreements, which, Harris writes, will produce a "net positive contribution to well-being," a "compassionate view of our common humanity," and a promotion of "the public good."[19]

According to Kitcher, as humans evolved, our hunting-gathering ancestors struggled with social conflicts over the inequitable distributions of tasks and resources when some of the more selfish of them failed to act altruistically and did not share with others. Social life in such small bands was fragile, so survival required that such social conflicts be resolved. The social structures of hunting-gathering tribes were highly egalitarian, Kitcher writes, so resolutions were worked out by everyone together, collectively, around the campfire, in ways that benefited everyone. An evolved capacity for psychological altruism expressed itself in established social norms of equal cooperation and sharing—resulting in functional cultures of fraternity, social solidarity, and altruism. Humans eventually began to internalize these norms and so feel guilty when they violated them. As civilizations developed, gods and religion were invented to justify and enforce these codes. Even if in today's modern world we realize no gods exist, we can and must nevertheless embrace strong norms of moral goodness, Kitcher says. That is partly because it is simply our human inheritance and nature, and partly because moral norms enable us to overcome selfish temptations and practice the altruism needed to avoid social conflict and promote social harmony.

Bayer and Figdor's approach is simpler. In reality, they say, no moral truths or rules or laws in nature or in objective reality exist. Whatever moral beliefs we have are pure human inventions. They even write: "there's no absolute moral code that dictates that murder is unethical."[20] Nonetheless, they observe, everyone does want to be happy. A simple fact of life is that all people both do and should "behave in ways that we think optimize our life happiness." There are many ways to be happy, both good and bad. Morality, then, is a matter of choosing to align one's own happiness with that of others. What it *means* to be moral, Bayer and Figdor stipulate, is to decide to make one's own happiness contingent upon the happiness of others. "A person can be said to act in a moral manner," as they define the term, "if he or she derives a great deal of self-happiness from other people's happiness." This view should motivate "balancing what you want against what's best for everyone," "identification with others," finding "happiness in observing the happiness of others," "wanting what's good for" others, choosing "to help others find happiness," and behaving ethically and supporting an ethical society.

Finally, Epstein similarly assumes that humans only have their own needs and interests to work with, nothing else. "Our morality," he says, "is based on human needs and social contracts."[21] And our ultimate human need or interest is to flourish. Ethics tell us how to live in ways that will promote flourishing. We also know that we value our own lives. Therefore, Epstein says, "logic commits us to universalize from there" to overcome selfishness and live in ways to respect the dignity of all people. "The dignity of mutual concern and connection and of self-fulfillment through service to humanity's highest ideals is more than enough reason to be good without God," he writes.[22]

These arguments contain some solid and admirable features[23]—but also a host of problems, including dubious premises, slippages of reasoning, and ignored counterclaims, which I could elaborate if necessary. For present purposes, I will limit myself to examining just a few crucial problems in these arguments.

THE PROBLEM OF UNJUSTIFIED EGALITARIAN UNIVERSALISM

The first problem for these atheistic moralists is that none of them provides a convincing reason—sometimes *any* reason—for the *universal* scope of humans' asserted obligations to promote the good of all other human beings. It is one thing for people to be good to those who are proximate and similar to them. It is quite another to demand that every person is morally obliged to advance the well-being of every other human on earth. A careful reading of our moralists reveals good reasons why atheists should be motivated to be good to a limited set of people who matter to them. But they do *not* provide good reasons to be good to everyone.

That these atheist moralists do champion universal, egalitarian, and inclusive moral standards is clear. Philip Kitcher is the most insistent among them. He writes that "a world counts as good to the extent actualizing it would lead us toward Utopia," that is, an "imaginary social state" in which "*each member* of the human population has a serious chance of living a good life" and where "the chances of living such lives are *equal across the population*."[24] "Almost *all* human beings," he says, "can advance from a state in which the good life is understood in terms of the satisfaction of basic needs . . . to a condition in which a richer conception of the good life makes sense for them." "My secular ideal," he thus writes, "commits itself to making available to *all* people the human possibilities proliferated by the ethical project."[25]

Similarly, Epstein writes: "We [humanists] are committed to treating *each person* as having inherent worth and dignity." Everyone must make "a decision together—not just as a family, clan, tribe, city, nation, or bloc of nations, but *as the human species*. We must decide, *all of us together*, to survive." Epstein endorses the Humanist Manifesto III of 2003, which encourages all to "aspire to the greater good of humanity" and "ground values in human welfare . . . extended to the global" level, in the "hope of attaining peace, justice, and opportunity for *all*," so that "*as many as possible* can enjoy a good life."[26] Though with less insistence than Kitcher and Epstein, Sam Harris too aspires to an inclusive universalism: "I want," he declares, "to live in a society that maximizes the possibility of human wellbeing *generally*," and we need to "succeed in building a *global* civilization based on shared values."[27]

Among these atheist moralists, only Bayer and Figdor equivocate about universalism. They hedge their language about how far our goodness ought to extend, in part by using ambiguous phrases, such as "our own happiness and . . . the happiness of others" (which

and how many others?), "our life-happiness" ("ours" individually or collectively?), and "the greatest life happiness for people
in society" (which people and which society?).[28] In a chapter
(claiming to be) about "how inclusive a society should be," they
conclude rather uncertainly that "we benefit from living in and
supporting an ethical society. . . . Ethical societies benefit *everyone*
because it is easier to live a happier life when you are surrounded
by other people who value cooperation and take pleasure in your
happiness." Unclear here is who counts as "we" and whether "society" means only that of a region or nation or more. (Moreover,
the claim is only about conditional benefits to cooperators, not
morally binding obligations to others.) Beyer and Figdor also explicitly concede naturalistic evolution's limitations on egalitarian
universalism:

> Research as far back as the work of Charles Darwin has shown
> that we are generally motivated to care more strongly for
> our families and our close social groups. The circle of caring
> then radiates outward to include people in our surrounding
> communities, states, and countries [though with limits]. . . .
> Why don't we treat everyone exactly the same? It's simple: we
> invest more energy in relationships that have a higher likelihood
> of benefiting us. . . . Treating everyone exactly equally is not how
> we are incentivized to behave. . . . This isn't a flaw but an evolved
> feature of the human mind. . . . [Our closer relationships mor-
> ally] *require us* to treat the other person in the relationship . . . *dif-
> ferently* from strangers.

So two of these atheist moralists are strong and inclusive moral
universalists (Kitcher and Epstein), one appears to be or at least
does not deny that approach (Harris), and the fourth pair is

more circumspect.[29] What arguments, then, do the two strong universalists provide to justify their positions?

Kitcher's argument runs like this: if *you* want to live a good life, to enjoy your own well-being (which you do), then you should realize that *other* people also want to live good lives and enjoy well-being. The human ethical project has always been about enhancing personal and social well-being. The more humans can live good lives, the better. Therefore, morality compels each person to commit to providing the conditions of well-being to every other person. To quote him: "almost all human beings want a future in which the younger members of their societies . . . can grow healthily. . . . [But] today the actions of people in some areas of the world [pollution, global warming] interfere with the re-alization of such desires." Therefore, "continuation of the eth-ical project should include an attempt to frame a conception of the common good responsive to the desires of *the entire human population*. . . . We urgently need a conception of the good that considers the desires of *all* people. . . . Where there are serious consequences for distant others, there *must* be an attempt to re-spond to them."[30]

Epstein's justification of moral universalism consists of four sentences referring to (without footnoting) the philosopher Rebecca Goldstein's reference to the philosopher Thomas Nagel, who argues in his book *The Possibility of Altruism* that "logic commits us to universalize . . . certain natural attitudes that already commit us to valuing our own lives." That is, we can reason that "we all know for ourselves that there is a right or wrong . . . so from there only radical selfishness could prevent us from understanding that these concepts are universal." (Here we appear to return to the Kantian view of having a "good reason" for acting morally, noted above and discussed in note 6.) And, Epstein says, since selfishness leads to unhappiness (which shifts back to a consequentialist ethics), that is not an option. Hence universalism. "Ethics really isn't that complicated," Epstein concludes.[31]

Neither Kitcher's nor Epstein's arguments for universalism is remotely persuasive. They may "convince" people who, for other (good or bad) reasons, *already want to* believe in inclusive moral universalism without thinking too hard about it. But convincing people who are already or mostly convinced is not the challenge. The challenge is to convince reasonable skeptics. So let us consider the position of a reasonable skeptic whose starting point is something like this: "I can see why, even without God, and understanding moral norms to be mere human inventions, I should be motivated to behave ethically and be good to the people around me who could affect my well-being. Beyond them, however, I see no compelling obligation to promote the well-being of other people who are irrelevant for all practical purposes to my own life, happiness, and welfare."

What can Kitcher and Epstein say to such a skeptic? Kitcher would reply: "but don't you see that those other distant people have the same aspirations and desires as you do? What you want for yourself they deserve equally too." I imagine the skeptic would ask: "why should I care about their aspirations and desires? Dealing with my own life is hard enough. Charity begins at home. I cannot be responsible for what everybody deserves. They and their people can take care of themselves." Kitcher answers: "but that is unfair! They also belong to our common humanity, as we benefit together from following moral norms. You have an obligation to help them and every other person." To which the skeptic replies: "says who? Anyway, life isn't fair—get used to it. If morality only exists to benefit us, then I will be moral with people I wish to benefit and who might benefit me."

What can Kitcher say? "You are a bad and selfish man"? No, that is desperate name-calling. What Kitcher needs but does not possess is a compelling argument, good reasons that could actually persuade the reasonable skeptic to be motivated to care about *all* other people. Kitcher does not have such reasons because his morally demanding inclusive and egalitarian universalism does not follow from his atheist, naturalist, functionalist premises. There remains a disconnect; there is no logical link between them. The reasonable skeptic sees that. Kitcher's metaphysics and moral ontology probably do justify the moral approach taken by the reasonable skeptic, but they do not justify the obligations Kitcher himself wishes to lay upon a secular society.[32]

If Kitcher's argument does not succeed, Epstein's fails miserably. His actually is not even an argument; instead it is a placeholder that dodges the problem. "Trust me," Epstein essentially says; "Goldstein and Nagel are really good philosophers and they have got this covered—logic forces us to universalize our own experience. It's really not complicated." Anyone who doubts, he suggests, is guilty of "radical selfishness" (more name-calling)—and needlessly overcomplicating ethics. Epstein's brevity and dismissiveness suggest either that he does not grasp the gravity of the issue at stake or that he intuitively senses the weakness of his position and nervously wishes quickly to change the subject. He has made not a dent in the position of the reasonable skeptic who accepts the value of socially bounded moral commitments and behaviors but sees no reason for accepting demanding, egalitarian, universal obligations.[33]

Universally inclusive systems of moral obligations are extremely tall orders that are very difficult if not impossible to fill. They require us to respect the (alleged) "dignity" of all people, not just nice and good people but also the most damaging, costly, ungrateful, and irredeemable people on the planet.[34] They expect us to identify and empathize with the needs and sufferings of every person, even those on the other side of the earth whose cultures are alien to ours. And we are to devote to them not merely passing sympathetic feelings but understanding, material aid, and resources. When we follow the Golden Rule, the "others" whom we "do unto" as we want done to ourselves are not only the friends and strangers with whom we interact, but everyone out there, from every social class, race, ethnicity, religion, political persuasion, country, and continent. Being good also requires, at least for Kitcher, more than sending donations to faraway victims of earthquakes, tsunamis, epidemics, and other disasters. It means the world's privileged proactively redistributing material resources and social services to ensure that everyone on the planet possesses an equal opportunity for well-being.

If human beings are to be asked to do these things, they will, given the demands involved, *have* to hear *really strong and persuasive reasons* clearly justifying them, involving both reasoned explanations and compelling motivations for moral living.[35] Yet these atheist moralists have none to offer that a reasonable skeptic cannot easily shrug off. They simply make assertions as if an inclusive, egalitarian universalism is the obvious next step in shared human progress, in "service to our highest ideals," the "uncomplicated" and inexorable outcome of the dutiful exercise of Kantian practical reason. But this is just wishful thinking, an evasion of reason.[36]

What ought we to conclude on this point about being "good without God?" I think that atheists are rationally justified in being morally good, if that means a modest goodness focused primarily on people who might affect them and with a view to practical consequences in terms of "enlightened self-interest." "Good," however, has no good reason to involve *universal* moral obligations. Atheists who wish to promote being "good without God," if they are intellectually honest, need to scale back their ambitions and propose something more defensible, forthright, and realistic than what most of these moralists seem to want. A more modest goodness may or may not suffice for functional human societies and a happy life, but—unless these atheist moralists have so far missed a big reason yet to be unveiled—that is all it seems atheism can rationally support.

THE PROBLEM OF THE "SENSIBLE KNAVE"

The second problem in the arguments of these atheistic moralists is that none of them successfully explains why rational persons in an atheistic universe should uphold a culture's moral norms *all* of the time. Why not be good when it serves one's enlightened self-interest but strategically choose to *break* a moral norm at opportune moments, when violation has a nice payoff and there is little chance of being caught?

You may be familiar with the history of this question. It is known as "Glaucon's challenge" to Socrates, recorded in Plato's *Republic*, and it is the problem of David Hume's "sensible knave," addressed in his *Enquiry Concerning the Principles of Morals*. (Today we might call Hume's sensible knave a "shrewd opportunist.") Neither Socrates nor Hume successfully resolved this problem,[37] and neither do today's atheist moralists. In fact, only one of the latter even confronts the challenge directly. The others either raise the question briefly and brush it aside, as if it is trivial; or else float some version of Socrates and Hume's (unsuccessful) answers and then hurriedly move on. In the end, Glaucon's challenge and Hume's "sensible knave" continue to stare all of their claims in the face, waiting for a more convincing answer. One will not be forthcoming, because there is no more convincing answer to bring forward.

Recall our atheistic situation. There is no objective, external source of moral order, such as God or a natural law. Humans invent morality through learning and social contract to make society function better—to benefit themselves. People are motivated to follow their culture's moral norms because breaking them will lead to punishment in the short run and unhappiness and reduced well-being in the longer run. This kind of enlightened self-interest should produce societies of people who are morally good without God.

But the fact is that, if this is indeed our situation, there is no good reason for perceptive and intelligent persons not to act as Hume's sensible knave, as shrewd opportunists, if they so desire. In fact, the more intelligent such persons are, the more they will want *other* people to follow all of the moral codes consistently, while they themselves opt to violate them when it is in their enlightened self-interest to do so. Let everyone else, who is not so clever, do the work of upholding the moral norms. To use the economist's language, many perceptive people in an atheist universe will be tempted on occasion to "free ride"—that is, let others pay the full fare for the collective benefits of moral order, while they themselves occasionally jump the turnstile while nobody is looking and ride for free.[38] To these reasonable arguments these atheist moralists have no good reply.[39] Thus, we cannot avoid concluding that "the imperfect coincidence of morality and self-interest implies that immorality need not always be irrational."[40]

Let us return to the details of the argument. The traditional reply to Glaucon's challenge and the sensible knave is to argue that immoral behavior inevitably inflicts psychological damage on the immoral one, disturbing his mental tranquility and generating anxiety about being caught. So the mere desire to enjoy peace of mind and satisfaction with one's own moral integrity should suffice to motivate everyone (except already morally corrupt reprobates) to be consistently morally good and never to "free ride."[41] How do these atheist moralists reply?

Only one of them, Philip Kitcher, addresses the problem directly. And in the end he admits to having no answer against the sensible knave.[42] Kitcher begins with the traditional answer, saying we should tell the sensible knave that "he will be disturbed and worried, that he will forfeit that tranquility of mind that good conscience bestows," and that he will also not actually achieve his goals.[43] But, Kitcher acknowledges, "in many instances, these responses will be ineffective." He then suggests telling the knave that his ability to take advantage of the moral system depends unfairly upon hard-won inherited moral systems and "the obedient docility of [his] fellows" upholding them. Kitcher knows, however, that the knave will reply that "this is all past history" and that "he is grateful so many of his predecessors went along with the codes" of morality so that "he can take advantage of that fact and pursue his egoistic goals." Kitcher (rightly) admits that a Kantian appeal to our duty to be consistent with rational principles is "powerless to prevent the [knave's] shrug. Who should care?" In the end, he admits that the "knave cannot be silenced" and that his own moral argument can do little more than "offer a diagnosis of what [knave] is doing"—namely, "the knavish incoherence" is taking advantage of the moral inheritance of humanity "that sustains human cooperation" and the good behavior of others. Quite so. Still, Kitcher concludes that the knave "shrugs his shoulders, unmoved by the rhetoric." In a last effort at self-defense, Kitcher claims that no other available moral system is able to answer the knave any better than he can. He then moves on to another topic.

As a moral philosopher, Kitcher is professionally the most qualified among these atheist moralists to solve this problem. Yet by his own admission he cannot provide a satisfactory reason why sensible knaves should not carefully free ride morally at the expense of others who are more cooperative and gullible. And if Kitcher cannot, there is no chance that Epstein, Harris, or the others can. And in fact they don't.

Imagine that you own a computer firm whose work involves protecting highly sensitive information. Imagine that you are approached by a salesperson offering a new data security program that provides full security against honest computer users; the only problem, this salesperson admits, is that the program also unfortunately has an irreparable systemic security hole that is vulnerable to being breached and exploited by malicious hackers. Do you want to buy this program? You should not. For you do not need to protect your sensitive data against honest users, but malicious hackers. This by analogy is the problem besetting the "good without God" moral systems that Kitcher and his fellow moralists are selling. They may work properly among well-intentioned people who uphold moral norms, but they are systematically and irremediably vulnerable to violation by sensible knaves.

Worse: the more sensible the knaves, the more vulnerable the moral systems are; and the more knaves exist who understand these systems' vulnerabilities, the more often they will be breached and people will not be good. Further, since these moral systems are "public goods," like subway systems, which remain functional only insofar as they are widely supported by "full-fare-paying riders," they are also vulnerable to delegitimation and possibly breakdown when a critical mass of sensible knaves behave in exploitive ways that the proponents of the moral systems cannot prevent with convincing reasons. And those I take to be debilitating problems for any "good without God" moral system.

Also note this ironic difficulty that the problem of sensible knaves generates for atheist moralists: it commends on pragmatic functional grounds popular ignorance instead of enlightenment about the facts of morality. For any enlightened atheist, preferring ignorance over illumination of the truth is perverse. Yet if atheism is correct, human practices of ethics will function more effectively if the general public remains in obfuscated darkness about morality's mere human origins and sheer functional purposes. People who believe that their moral norms reflect objective standards of moral truth—what philosophers call "moral facts"—will be more likely to uphold them than people who see that they are mere human constructions that evolved to reduce social conflicts and enhance general human well-being. The Great and Terrible Oz of morality, so to speak, was only revered and obeyed when the denizens of Oz paid "no attention to that man behind the curtain." When he is revealed to the masses as just a humbug man with a hot-air balloon from Omaha, the dykes holding back sensible knavery will be breached. Thus, ironically, moral education will not promote greater moral living but increased moral skepticism and knavery. Therefore, to minimize that threat, better for those in charge of social order to allow and even encourage people to believe the myths that morality is based in God or natural law or karma or whatever else the atheists are debunking. It would be better for a "good without God" world to be populated by misled conformists than enlightened knaves— because the former will be more likely to be consistently good, even when they have no good reason to be. That is a perverse bind for atheists, who claim to be our greatest champions of enlightened intelligence, scientific realism, and education in the facts.

Furthermore, these atheist moralists have not eliminated from their moral systems the judging and punishing God they so loathe and wish to eradicate; they have simply substituted for a religious God the punishing god of "society." Nobody suggests that people will voluntarily behave morally without the threat of sanctions.

Every moral system under consideration, atheist and otherwise, recognizes that the monitoring, judgments, rewards, and punishment of some kind of superindividual power are necessary to enforce compliance. Getting rid of God does not change that; it just shifts the burden of behavior regulation to the informal and formal social-control functions of human society: surveillance, gossip, snitching, state regulations, police forces, courts, prisons, and so on. Even people motivated by an enlightened self-interest in increasing their own well-being also need the fear of punishment to inform their calculations. Bayer and Figdor frame this fact nicely: "the choice to be a comparatively moral person is easier in the context of a society with well-considered ethical laws, since breaking these laws will usually fail to optimize a person's life-happiness. In other words, laws often set up an incentive structure that aligns individual self-interest with behavior that benefits society at large." But the harsher reality also emerges: "that's why we often reinforce ethical values when we see others straying by . . . publicly *shaming* them."[44] And when it comes to society's powers of social control, public shaming is only the beginning. Likewise, for Kitcher egalitarian hunter-gatherers collectively agreed upon moral norms, but those who might violate them were necessarily threatened with punishments and social exclusion: "behind [morality] must stand practices of punishment. Unless there were sanctions for disobedience, fear could hardly be central to the initial capacity for normative guidance. Conversely, when punishment is present in a group, it can make possible the evolution of elaborate forms of cooperative behavior."[45] Hence the importance of the risk of being caught in wrongdoing and having one's reputation ruined.[46] Atheists scorn the idea of a punishing God who induces fearful obedience, but in the end they must substitute their own version of the same, a watchful and punishing human society, to secure moral order. So if anyone thinks "good without God" means a system in which oversight, control, and punishment are eliminated in favor of widespread voluntary expressions of ethical behavior, she will be waiting forever. The choice between God and (social) god, between one's creator and judge and the myriad social control mechanisms of society, is inescapable.

Finally, Kitcher claims that his "diagnosis seems no worse than that offered by the major rival approaches to ethics."[47] While this is not the main point of this chapter, I must beg to differ. Does belief in God *guarantee* that everyone will always do the right thing? Of course not. There are plenty of religious knaves. However, I *do* think that certain kinds of theisms (if their premises are granted) *do* at least provide *good reasons* for avoiding knavery, better than those Kitcher can offer. One is that God loves us and knows better than we do what is best for us even in this life, and so, even when we are tempted to do wrong for our own advantage, we have a good reason to believe that we will be better off in the long run to do what is right instead, however difficult that is. (Note: this is not an argument from divine command, which atheists, I think misguidedly, believe is indefensible, but from divine benevolence and trustworthiness.) A second reason is that, while we sensible knaves may be able to fool the people around us, we cannot fool an all-knowing God, and will in time (by many religious accounts) certainly be judged and punished for wrongdoing and rewarded for good deeds. Those two religiously based reasons and others besides may not constrain all knaves, given the immense human capacity for knavery, but (when their premises are granted) they *do* present *good reasons* why knaves *should* constrain their wrongdoing—reasons that are unavailable to atheists. So there *are* differences in systems of moral reasoning on this point, Kitcher's claim to the contrary notwithstanding.

Now, to be clear, returning to my main argument, I am not advocating that everyone in an atheist universe *should* morally free ride or *ought* to become sensible knaves. Many people may well choose to abide consistently by their culture's moral norms. My point is simply that nobody in an atheist universe confronts a good reason *not* to free ride morally under the right conditions, if they so desire, because atheist moralists do not possess such a good reason. Kitcher knows that, and the other moralists have just ignored it. But the problem of moral free riding and sensible knaves is not trivial. Indeed, as far as I can tell, a lot of people in our world today actually do live by a sensible-knave strategy and do not seem driven by their psychological misery back into a consistent upholding of moral norms. If we are to move into a future that is intent on being "good without God," these morally corrosive facts, this systemic vulnerability to moral hackers must be acknowledged and our moral expectations adjusted accordingly. Again, I say, atheists have reasons to be good without God, but not as faithfully and consistently good as these atheist moralists would like us to think.

THE EVADED DIFFICULTY OF CONFLICTING INTERESTS

Underlying both problems examined above is the more general fact that *individual and collective interests often conflict.* This remains true even after human self-interest is fully "enlightened." The tension between the two in real life cannot be dissolved. What serves the apparent well-being of specific persons (and the people they care about) in various situations frequently differs from what is best for the larger group. Every culture has ways to try to blunt the edges of this difficult tension, to make the two sets of interests as compatible as possible. But the tension cannot be resolved.

These atheist moralists explicitly recognize this conflict from time to time. Sam Harris, for instance, observes in one place that "we are not, by nature, impartial—and much of our moral reasoning must be applied to situations in which there is a tension between our concern for ourselves, or for those closest to us, and our sense that it would be better to be more committed to helping others." He also writes: "it often seems impossible to determine whose well-being should most concern us."[48] But rarely do our moralists try to explain how this problem might be overcome, and never do they do so successfully. In the end, they gloss over the problem. They must, for when it is engaged directly and fully, their arguments break down.

Why so? A crucial hinge on which the arguments of these atheist moralists turn is the close association between what is good for the individual and what is good for other people. They say that people are essentially motivated to enhance their own happiness and well-being, and that moral norms are socially generated to facilitate that. But moral norms also require that enlightened individuals *constrain* some of what would serve their immediate self-interests in order to serve the interests of the group, and thereby serve their own long-term self-interests indirectly. So, the closer an individual's self-interest aligns with the interests of all others, the less individuals have to constrain themselves—meaning, the easier it is for them to be moral (which for our moralists means being good to other people), because everyone's interests come close to coinciding. No tension, no conflict, no problem. If the interests of individuals and of everyone else were identical, the problem of motivating people to be good would disappear. Everyone could simply pursue their own personal interests, happiness, and well-being, and that pursuit would inherently involve being good to and for everyone else.

Yet the more individual and collective interests diverge, the harder it is to explain why individuals—who now think that their only real moral motivation is to be happy and enjoy well-being[49]—should avoid doing what is good for themselves in order to serve the good of all.[50] Enlightened self-interest can reduce the distance between the conflicting interests, but at some point, it falls short. In order to persuade readers that everyone can readily be good without God, these atheist moralists have a compelling reason to downplay conflicts between individual and collective interests. By my reading, they seem highly motivated to sidestep the problem.

One way to do so is simply to dissolve the problem by definitional fiat. Bayer and Figdor, for instance, define "morality" itself by conflating personal and social interests. "A person can be said to act in a moral manner," they write in a crucial passage, "if he or she derives a great deal of self-happiness from other people's happiness. A person acts immorally if he or she derives little happiness from the happiness of others. . . . With that definition, we *remove the requirement of selflessness* from morality and focus our attention on what really matters—identifying with others and wanting good for them."[51] Lovely. When everyone's happiness aligns, life is splendid; we don't need to think about the costs of being good. But the authors are simply evading the cases when one is made *un*happy by what makes others happy, when individual and collective interests do *not* align. Then, in the later chapter promising to sort these issues out, Bayer and Figdor only get lost in a discussion of the trolley problem and musings about some of their own ethical opinions, finally concluding that "all our beliefs are subject to change in the face of new evidence." The key difficulty remains unaddressed.

Another way these atheist moralists dodge this problem is rhetorically to confuse what is possible or typical with what is necessarily true. Harris writes: "our selfish and selfless interest *do not always* conflict."[52] True, but *sometimes they do*, and that is the problem at stake. Bayer and Figdor claim that "pursuing [one's own] happiness . . . can and do[es] lead to 'typical' moral behavior" in part because "enlightened self-interest [means that] prioritizing your own concerns can lead you to behave in a way that is moral and beneficial for society."[53] True again. But just because it *can* lead to that does not mean that it always will or should. They also write: "we choose to act morally because our personal preferences are to act in that way. And since those personal preferences *so often line up* with societal morality . . . we end up with an uncomplicated conclusion: We choose to be moral because of the happiness it brings us." Maybe, sometimes. But, again, what about when personal preferences do *not* "line up" with societal morality? About that they have little to say.[54]

Yet another rhetorical strategy to avoid the problem of conflicting personal versus social interests is appealing to extremes that offer obvious conclusions but sidestep the problem. Harris observes that "there is often a tension between the autonomy of the individual and the common good" but then follows with "the fact that it might be difficult to decide *exactly* how to balance individual rights against collective interests . . . does not mean that there aren't objectively *terrible* ways of doing this."[55] *Of course* there are terrible ways of doing that, but how does that point help us deal with the real problem? Similarly, Epstein argues that "if I am *only* for myself" then I will personally suffer "dire consequences" that will make me unhappy.[56] True enough. But the problem is not about people *only* being for themselves. Even the sensible knave is never *only* for himself. Such extremes are not in question here, and raising them only obfuscates the difficulties these atheist moralists should be confronting.[57]

In the end, our moralists sidestep rather than work through the fact that individual interests (including the interests of other people an individual knows and cares about) and collective interests often conflict. Failing to resolve that difficulty means they are also unable to explain why reasonable atheists ought to be committed to a universal humanism and refrain from sensible knavery.

NAÏVE CREDULITY ABOUT NATURAL HUMAN GOODNESS

A second underlying problem besetting the claims of these atheist moralists, which is also implicated in the problems discussed above, is their *tendency to assume a naïvely optimistic view of human nature.* Much in their writings seems highly motivated to suppress the recognition of darkness in human experience. Their books occasionally acknowledge humanity's history of and capacity for evil. For example, Kitcher mentions the human "record of cruelty and indifference," "the old disease—the limited ability of human beings to perceive and accommodate one another," "self-destructive urges," and "deep resentment and hatred of others."[58]

But those occasions are overwhelmed by larger arguments that presuppose human beings as quite reasonable, cooperative, well-intentioned, and good. Nearly all of these atheist moralists' writings exhibit a breezy Enlightenment confidence in social contracts and moral progress. Their faith in our capacity to put humanity's darkness in the past—especially if we can get rid of religion and build the secular new society—is boundless. Kitcher, for instance, responds to his own observation that "people have done appalling things to one another" with this reassuring warning against "blind acceptance of powerful [religious] myths": "the convictions underlying pessimism of this sort [e.g., belief in "original sin"] do not stem from rigorously grounded forms of psychological understanding or from scientific evidence about the inevitable eruption of dark tendencies under a wide range of social environments. . . . Judgments about the ineradicability of hypothetical human tendencies are premature."[59]

How exactly is this fault implicated in the problems examined above? The answer is clear. If humans are basically reasonable, cooperative, well-intentioned, and good, then it will be much easier to imagine them cheerfully building a secular world of universal freedom, equality, fraternity, and dignity—and a society untroubled by sensible knaves. Likewise, good humans will be well-equipped to minimize conflicts between individual and collective interests. In short, the more naturally good humans are thought to be, the easier being "good without God" becomes.

Thus, nearly everything these atheist moralists discuss concerns how very possible and reasonable it is for people to be good. That of course is the core message of their books. But to be convincing, they would need to engage much more with the overwhelming empirical evidence that humans often have been and are *not* good—as assessed not theologically but by the atheists' own normative standards—and that most social experiments to expunge badness from humanity have consistently failed and sometimes brought forth even greater evils.

Their optimism about humanity is more evident in what these atheist moralists *fail to say* than in what they explicitly articulate. Their near total silence about our tortured and blood-sodden experience makes their works read like utopian fantasies. Optimism about human potential is more assumed than argued. Only occasionally does that general confidence surface in direct form. In one such instance, Epstein offers as one of his general life rules the belief that "Nice Guys Do Finish First."[60] Really? As a rule this is clearly empirically false. Sometimes nice people finish first, and sometimes, perhaps often, they don't.

At one point Bayer and Figdor try to explain why people should stop "the sad tendency to dehumanize anyone who is different from us."[61] They take as an instructive case study the 2013 Boston Marathon bombing committed by the brothers Dzhokhar and Tamerlan Tsarnaev, whom they reprove for espousing "a deeply misguided form of Islam." (Why exactly—having both dismissed all religions as false and relegated all judgments of objective truth to mere personal opinions—Bayer and Figdor believe they are in a position to declare which forms of Islam are authentic and misguided is beyond my comprehension, but that is another matter.) How do Bayer and Figdor think such terrorist behavior could be prevented? Their solution is to try to use reason to persuade aspiring terrorists not to kill others: "if I had been able to confront the brothers before they acted, I would have tried to reason with them. I would have explained why the bombings would not be in their own self-interest nor in the long-term interest of their cause . . . to convince them that their worldview . . . is not conducive to creating life-happiness for themselves and the society they live in."[62] I too would like to see noncoercive reasoning do as much good work in the world as possible. But to think that sitting down with terrorists and other "bad" people and appealing to their enlightened self-interest in happiness will change their minds and turn them into "good" people is extremely naïve—and not because of any religious doctrine of original sin but because such an expectation is so far removed from the facts about how many people in the real world actually think, feel, and operate.

Epstein writes: "we can agree on certain things we don't want to see happen: such as another holocaust or genocide."[63] While that is true of many people, it can only with the greatest innocence—arguably self-deceived ignorance—be taken as the consensus of humanity. Every decade since the last world war has witnessed blood-soaked genocides in various parts of the world, including Europe. And neo-Nazism, right-wing nationalisms, anti-Semitism, and similarly dark forces have hardly disappeared from the earth— as of this writing, if anything, they appear to be on the rise. The confidence with which Epstein congratulates "us" on our morality is unwarranted.

Or take as a further example this statement of another atheist moralist, Katherine Ozment: "I've always believed that people are basically good—they just need structures in their lives to reinforce that goodness. . . . I suspect we all live by some version of treating others well."[64] Really? I see little evidence in history or the contemporary world for the idea that all people live by the rule that they should treat others well. These atheists' naïveté about humanity simply cannot serve as the basis for a realistic moral philosophy.

In short, the picture of humanity that atheist moralists paint is too bright, too sanguine, too confident. It is not my purpose to expound on the dark aspects of human nature. But it must be observed that absent from these works is any recognition of human history's *tragic* quality, to which (not only religious) human literature, drama, philosophy, and social commentary have testified for millennia. These works barely note the seemingly endemic and recurrent human capacities for evil, destruction, and self-destruction, despite the overwhelming evidence of them that bears upon us every day. Never registered in these pages are the writings of the many secular intellectuals who have compellingly advanced bleak antihumanist accounts of our human condition. (Epstein's kid-glove account of Nietzsche is remarkable: "he cannot be entirely absolved for the fact that some of [his] sound bites suggest, whether he meant them or not, that the strong and fortunate have no moral obligation to the weak and powerless.")[65] From start to finish, these atheist moralists seem intent on downplaying the egoistic, selfish, acquisitive, tribal, violent, and sadistic sides of human experience.

This cheerful picture of humanity further reflects a failure to grasp how culturally relative are the affective responses to human pain and destruction that "people" (as if humanity is all the same) experience. Humans can be socialized to react in many ways to violence and pain among members of out-groups. In some cultures, people grimace and show pity over harm or pain inflicted on fellow humans; in others, they are impassive or even cheer and laugh. Yet these atheist moralists assume that people universally feel good about "prosocial" experiences and recoil at the suffering and ruin of others. That again is wishful thinking. Brains must be formed to respond to such experiences, and instinctive human tendencies toward empathy can be readily overridden. It is common to see as normal the infliction of barbarism, humiliation, and suffering on people beyond one's own. Truly inclusive, empathetic humanism is the exception. These atheist moralists have inherited a particular humanistic moral tradition formed by millennia of ethical influences, including religious ones, which they are credulous and ill-informed to take for granted as a human universal.[66]

Optimism about humanity pervades these works for a number of reasons. One is these atheists' vehement opposition to religious doctrines of "original sin" and "total depravity," which seems to drive them to opposite secular positions of original goodness and only-minor-and-unthreatening-depravity. Another is their selective representation of recent work in sociobiology and evolutionary psychology emphasizing the prosocial aspects of humanity's evolutionary inheritance, through mechanisms such as inclusive fitness, kinship selection, reciprocal altruism, and so on. A third reason may be the tendency of atheists generally to lay the blame for what is dark in humanity on the ignorance, superstitions, and malevolence of religion, which they believe can be overcome as secularism finally wins the day. An optimistic view of humanity is of course typical of Enlightenment liberals, whether secular or religious, who are deeply invested in the ideas of human progress, reason, and the transformative power of education. In any case, authors beckoning readers to affirm their capacity for moral goodness and the realization of "our highest ideals" without God cannot afford to dwell upon too dark a picture of the human condition. And these authors definitely do not.

But the imbalance backfires. It undercuts readers' trust in the authors and their arguments. Had these atheist moralists presented and worked with a more even-handed view of human moral capacities and tendencies, both dark and light, their cases might be more convincing—except that they would then be forced to change some of their arguments substantially. Instead, their conclusions feel more like whimsy than realistic analysis. They confuse the way our moralists *hope* people could be with how humans really are. The distinct impression one draws is that their cases for being "good without God" precariously depend on a credulous faith in an innate and reliable goodness of human beings.

This problem is also curiously ironic, since these very same atheist moralists represent a movement that fancies itself the vanguard of a no-nonsense, hard-nosed realism about our true human condition. "Just the facts of empirical science, please, with no illusions about God, the meaning of life, or objective moral truths." We are talking here about people who inform us, without batting an eye, that "there's no absolute moral code that dictates that murder is unethical."[67] Then these same authors turn around and, in explaining how to be good without God, espouse breezily optimistic ideas about human nature and moral potential, all but blind to our species' capacity for evil. The incongruity is perplexing.

CONCLUSION

I said in the introduction to this chapter that I began this inquiry with a genuinely open mind, interested to see if atheists really could make a solid case for the rational justification for a strong morality. I'm afraid I came away disappointed.[68]

"The question," Charles Taylor has asked, "is whether we are not living beyond our moral means in continuing allegiance to our [high] standards of justice and benevolence. Do we have ways of seeing-good which are still credible to us, which are powerful enough to sustain these standards? If not, it would be both more honest and more prudent to moderate them."[69] My conclusion about the atheist moralists examined above is that they are trying to live beyond their reasonable means and would be honest and prudent to moderate their claims.

The atheist moralists are overreaching. An ethics of genuine goodness without God may be possible. But the substantive obligations of such a morality are not what most activist atheists claim they can justify. They will need to lower their standards to fit the premises and parameters that their atheistic universe actually provides. People seem justified in being "moderately" good without God, motivated by a concern about the practical consequences of morality for their own and their loved ones' well-being, understood in terms of "enlightened self-interest" (what I have called a modest or moderate goodness). But rational and intellectually honest atheists do not have good reasons justifying their strong, inclusive, universalistic humanism, which requires all people to adhere to high moral norms and to share their resources in an egalitarian fashion for the sake of equal opportunity and the promotion of human rights.

Judging by their own accounts of their lives, most of these atheist moralists had pretty clear ideas of what was morally good, right, and just prior to committing to atheism. Some even admit that these ideas were religiously formed early in life. When they later became atheists, they then set out to reaffirm the core of their prior moral sensibilities and commitments in light of their beliefs in a godless universe. Their conclusions, in other words, were to some extent determined before they began to think and write— so it appears to me that they are reasoning to a strongly preferred conclusion, not a logically entailed conclusion. That is not the best way to work out a coherent moral philosophy, and it will not convince the reasonable skeptic. It seems to me to fall into the cognitive bias of what cognitive and social scientists call "motivated reasoning," that is, searching for evidence that confirms what one already believes and wants to continue believing, rather than rationally and even-handedly seeking information that could confirm or disconfirm a particular belief.[70] And that sets up some of our moralists to try to force and finesse arguments that in fact do not succeed.[71]

Still, mine is a qualified conclusion. I am not convinced, as are some religious people, along with (what is commonly attributed to) Dostoyevsky, that "if God does not exist, then all things are possible," or that an atheistic universe must unavoidably degenerate into Nietzschean nihilism.[72] I have come to think that a secular neo-Aristotelian virtues ethics can provide a more moderate, chastened approach that avoids the extremes of both Nietzschean nihilism and the overreaching optimism of new atheists yet is also broadly compatible with theism—about which more in the conclusion.[73] Meanwhile, my answer to the good-without-God question, in the end, is: to some significant extent, yes, humans can be and should be moderately good without God. But, please, don't get carried away with high expectations and stringent demands.

Chapter 2

Does Naturalism Warrant Belief in Universal Benevolence and Human Rights?

This chapter considers the kind of morality we would have reason to believe in if it was known to be the case that we inhabit a naturalistic universe.[1] In particular, I wish to consider whether in that case we would have reason to believe—as very many modern people in fact do—in universal benevolence and human rights as moral facts and imperatives.

A naturalistic universe is one that consists of energy and matter and other natural entities, such as vacuums, operating in a closed system in time and space, in which no transcendent, supernatural, divine being or superhuman power exists as creator, sustainer, guide, or judge. Such a universe has come to exist by chance—not by design or providence but by purposeless natural forces and processes. There is no inherent, ultimate meaning or purpose. Any meaning or purpose that exists for humans in a naturalistic universe is constructed by and for humans themselves. When the natural forces of entropy eventually extinguish the human race—if some natural or humanmade disaster does not do so sooner—there will be no memory or meaning, just as none existed before human consciousness evolved. This naturalistic universe is the background reality that mainstream natural science seems to tell us we inhabit. Officially, science is only *methodologically* naturalistic, not meta-physically so,[2] meaning that scientific methods and explanations only appeal to natural causes but science makes no judgments about the nature of ultimate reality. But many of science's spokespersons seem to assume and sometimes explicitly promote metaphysical naturalism as well (as I will show in the following chapter). At the very least, almost no mainstream science spokesperson advocates the existence of a supernatural reality transcending nature or imma-nent in it.[3] Metaphysical naturalism also describes the kind of uni-verse that most atheists insist we inhabit.[4]

Naturalism is not atheism. Metaphysical naturalism is a general picture of all reality as consisting of nothing but the operations of nature. Atheism, by comparison, is the specific, "not-theism" an-swer to the question of whether some kind of divine being exists. The two are logically related. In fact, most committed metaphysical naturalists are functional if not declared atheists, and vice versa. So while the two positions are distinct in the claims they make, they readily and usually go hand in hand. My explorations in this chapter frame matters not in terms of atheism specifically but in the broader but closely related terms of naturalism, in order to examine whether naturalism can provide sound justifications for a belief in universal benevolence and human rights.

What do I mean by universal benevolence and human rights? Many modern people tend to believe strongly that all human per-sons everywhere possess inalienable human rights to life, certain freedoms, respect of conscience, and protection against unwar-ranted or arbitrary violations of personal property and choices by government or other persons. The enjoyment of these rights, it is widely believed, is not contingent upon being smart, attractive, wealthy, strong, or any other conditional quality or situation. Simply being a human person endows one with such rights and entitles one to their respect by and justice from others. Such basic human rights are such that they place a moral duty on people to honor, protect, and defend not only their own rights but also the rights of other humans if they are able to do so.

Further, many modern people believe in universal benevolence, that is, belief in the inherent moral goodness of sustaining the lives, reducing the suffering, promoting the health, and increasing the well-being of other people, including strangers, and perhaps particularly of the weak and vulnerable. Again, in principle, benevolence is commonly believed valid for every person of both sexes in all nations, races, religions, social classes, and ethnicities. Whether other people are similar to us or not, it is widely believed, it is morally good to protect their lives and relieve their sufferings, simply because they are human.

Such beliefs may seem idealistic. But they are woven into the institutional and cultural fabric of many contemporary societies and the international system. It is because of the belief in universal benevolence and human rights that nations often come to the aid of distant disaster victims, hospitals try to save and improve the lives of even the most sick and diseased, and people give money to alleviate victims of famine, flood, and epidemics. It is ultimately because of these moral beliefs that the United Nations and many NGOs and individual advocates work, for example, to curtail the spread of AIDS in Africa and elsewhere, to provide clean drinking water to remote villages in the developing world, and to organize for the release of prisoners of conscience and the end of torture.

Such beliefs also often form the background against which many people try to treat others, including strangers and those who are different in various ways, with respect, courtesy, tolerance, and sometimes kindness. In fact, the ideas of universal benevolence and human rights have given rise to myriad important features of contemporary life, from the globally significant United Nations Universal Declaration of Human Rights to established legal protections afforded criminal suspects and to the heartsickness that many ordinary people feel on hearing news of disaster, injustice, and tragedy, even among strangers who live far away. In short, universal benevolence and rights are central features of the moral sensibilities of many—though not all—people today.

The question I address here is this: If we in fact live in the naturalistic cosmos that atheists and much of science tell us we occupy, do we have good reasons for believing in universal benevolence and human rights as moral facts and imperatives? In addressing the issues such a query raises, it is helpful to distinguish three different questions. The first is: Can and do people who believe that we live in a naturalistic universe also believe in universal benevolence and human rights and act upon such beliefs? The answer, obviously, is yes: many believers in naturalism are also passionate and devoted believers in human dignity, universal benevolence, and human rights. That answer is so clear, in fact, that simply asking the question risks insulting such people, though it is a point worth clarifying up front.

The second question is this: Do people who believe that we live in a naturalistic universe *have good reason* to believe in universal benevolence and human rights—that is, are they *rationally warranted* in asserting and championing such moral claims and imperatives? Asked differently: Does the moral belief in universal benevolence and human rights fit well with and flow reasonably from the facts of a naturalistic universe? This is the main question I address in this chapter.

The answer I will consider is this: no; if we are intellectually honest, we will see that a belief in universal benevolence and human rights as moral fact and obligation does not fit well with, or naturally flow from, the realities of a naturalistic universe. Someone who believes in a naturalistic cosmos is, it seems to me, perfectly entitled to believe in and act to promote universal benevolence and human rights, but only as an arbitrary, subjective, personal preference—*not* as a rational, compelling, universally binding fact and obligation. Persons who live in a naturalistic universe may certainly *choose* to affirm universal benevolence and human rights. But they might equally reasonably choose some other, quite different, or even radically different, moral position. At bottom, they do not occupy higher moral grounds for making compelling and binding claims on others on behalf of universal benevolence and human rights.[5] This may be an unpopular argument, and I may in fact be wrong, although I currently cannot see how or why. But if I am not wrong, then it seems to follow that many contemporary atheists, who operate with a background worldview of metaphysical naturalism, are overreaching in their claim that they are rationally justified in believing, on atheist terms, in universal benevolence and human rights.

The third question is: *If* my answer to the second question is correct—that intellectual honesty does not grant residents of a naturalistic universe warranted moral belief in universal benevolence and human rights—will human societies and cultures that want to believe in them anyway, for whatever reasons, be able, notwithstanding the lack of warrant, to sustain such beliefs over the long run? If my answer to the second question is in fact wrong, then this is not a concern. In that case, people who want human societies to affirm and institutionalize the belief in universal benevolence and human rights should be able to appeal to the reasonable warrant, the good fit, the natural inference that such beliefs represent in a naturalistic universe.

But if my answer to the second question is correct, then social practices grounded on belief in universal benevolence and human rights are endangered. In theory, they would be in grave danger. However, the third question is not about theory. It is about whether *in real practice, as human cultures and societies actually tend to function*, universal benevolence and human rights would in fact be jeopardized. The answer to this question is, it seems to me: maybe, maybe not. I think one can reasonably argue both ways. We simply may not be in a position to know until the answer is an accomplished fact one way or another. Sociological considerations tend to make me think that over time such beliefs will erode. But more on this later. First, I engage in depth the second question.

HISTORICAL TRANSCENDENT ACCOUNTS

I have said that I am inclined to believe that if we are intellectually honest we must concede that belief in universal benevolence and human rights as moral fact and obligation does not fit well with, does not reasonably flow from, the realities of a naturalistic universe. Perhaps it is worth mentioning that I actually do not wish this to be the case. Given the institutional authority of naturalism in modernity, especially in science, the future of human societies would be more securely like what I believe they should be morally—namely, institutionally committed to universal benevolence and human rights—if these did make reasonable sense in a naturalistic universe. But I do not see how they do. If anything, it appears to me that a naturalistic universe can naturally give rise to quite different moral

commitments, ones quite objectionable to those who believe in benevolence and rights.

But, if so, why or how is it that so many modern people do
appear to believe in universal benevolence and human rights?
Answering this (fourth) question is not the focus of this chapter, but
it does provide a key background assumption for my argument. The
best answer—one that many believers in naturalism recognize—
points us in a historical direction, toward the metaphysics and
moral teachings of religious traditions, particularly Judaism and
Christianity.

Many ancient civilizations and cultures readily accepted and
practiced different forms of slavery, infanticide, patriarchy, and sometimes human sacrifice. Many took for granted innate inequalities
between different groups of people. In general, few possessed the
cultural resources to develop a strongly humanistic morality of the
kind we widely affirm today.

By contrast, the transcendent monotheism of ancient Judaism
introduced a set of uncommon ethical sensibilities that were crucial in the eventual development of the culture of benevolence and
rights. These included Jewish sacred beliefs in all human persons
being made "in the image of God"; in God liberating the Hebrews
from oppressive Egyptian slavery; in Yahweh as a God of justice,
righteousness, and loving kindness; in Yahweh as the only true
God over all the people and nations of the earth (universalism);
and in the Promised Land as a place of abundance but also social
justice, economic equity, and judicial integrity. Yahweh abhorred
infanticide and human sacrifice, demanded justice for the poor,
and set legal limits on ill treatment of servants and criminals. Over
centuries, Judaism developed a keen self-critical consciousness
through recurrent prophetic condemnations of injustice, exploitation, and neglect of the poor, the needy, widows, strangers, aliens,

and the unjustly accused. Judaism also evolved a universal vision of God's chosen people on a mission not to conquer the nations but to serve as the people through whom all of the nations might come to know God's love and righteousness and so stream to God's throne to worship.

Christianity directly inherited this ethical legacy and added to it the demanding teachings of Jesus on love for one's enemies, universalizing the "neighbor," self-sacrificial giving, the disciples' worldwide mission, the sacred value of caring for the physical needs of others, and the dignity and importance of women, children, and "sinners." The Christian Apostles further taught the duty to share material wealth, respect for the consciences of others, the priority of persuasion over force, and the power of God's kingdom to dissolve divisive social distinctions—"in Christ there is neither Jew nor Greek, male nor female, slave nor free," Saint Paul declared; "all are one in Christ Jesus."[6]

Of course, both Jews and Christians have over millennia recurrently failed to live up to their own moral teachings—sometimes miserably so and with dreadful consequences. But Jewish and Christian teachings—on sin, repentance, forgiveness, and restitution—have also provided the grounds above and beyond "natural sentiments" for bad conscience, prophetic condemnation, penitence, and self-correction. And the moral teachings of these religious traditions—canonized in sacred scriptures and elaborated in the practices of religious communities—have through centuries of Jewish diaspora and Christendom been diffused and embedded as deep structures in the moral cultures of entire societies and civilizations. The skeptical Enlightenment and modernity shattered Christendom and largely disestablished Christianity. But the Enlightenment and modernity have also carried on and developed in mostly secular forms the long humanistic moral tradition launched and fostered by millennia of

Jewish and Christian tradition. That is, they have retained much of Christian and Jewish moral values and attempted to reestablish them on nontheistic footings.

In short, the widespread belief of many moderns—whether religious or not—in universal benevolence and human rights can be traced in large part to deep cultural roots in specific religious traditions that for millennia have nurtured a particular vision of universal human dignity, responsibility, and accountability. As a counterfactual matter—politically incorrect perhaps but I think nevertheless historically demonstrable—few ancient human cultures appear to have possessed the embryonic metaphysical and moral cultural material from which could have evolved the robust commitment to universal benevolence and human rights that many moderns today embrace. In any case, regardless of what might have otherwise developed with regard to benevolence and rights, in fact what actually *did* develop, at least in the West, was in large measure the cultural and institutional outcome of deep historical Jewish and Christian roots. And at the heart of those traditions was the belief in a transcendent personal God who is the source, governor, and judge of moral order and action.

Implicit in my account and relevant for the argument hereafter is my assumption that sustaining belief commitments to ideas and practices that are difficult and costly requires an account or narrative that satisfactorily explains to neophytes and doubters the reality and reasons behind the belief commitments themselves. Beliefs with demanding and challenging implications and consequences need at least implicit rationales in order for people to embrace and act on them over the long run. Such beliefs will not perpetuate themselves over time without justification. When skeptics ask why anyone should care about someone suffering on the other side of the world or in some hospital or foreign war zone, those who do believe that we all should care must have a good answer, a compelling account to offer. "Because each human person is made in the image of God" has been one historically compelling account, at least as long as people believed in God. Whether explanations such as "Because 'society' says so" and "You would wish others to care for you if you were suffering" might continue to serve as an effective account may be questionable.

Another premise of my argument worth surfacing here is that many people are not naturally and predominantly altruistic, self-giving, considerate of the needs of others, and more committed to truth and justice than their own welfare. This is not a grand position on philosophical anthropology but a general empirical observation that I think is defensible and relevant to this discussion. Most people have not only bright sides with capacities for genuine good but also dark sides with capacities for deep selfishness, self-deception, and indifference toward the needs of others. It is precisely this fact that helps generate in the first place the problem of benevolence and rights. If everyone were naturally so good, then we would not need to work so hard to justify and defend universal benevolence and rights.

I will address the second question posed above by taking the role of the skeptic who does not see why, if the universe is the natural-istic one science tells us it is, we should have a moral commitment to universal benevolence and human rights. Why should we not re-alize that such a commitment is grounded in an illusory religious metaphysics, reject that commitment as ill-informed, and formu-late alternative moral commitments that are more consistent with the real universe in which we actually live? I will put forward what seems to me an intellectually coherent and honest case based on naturalism, even at the expense of perhaps offending deeply held moral convictions and sensibilities.

NATURALISM AND MORALITY

Recall the features of a naturalistic universe. There is no transcendent natural law or moral force, no divinity, no ultimate spiritual meaning or destiny that transcends human invention during the blip of cosmic time that we humans have occupied. Reality consists of various conglomerations of infinitesimally small particles pulled together by physical forces and processes of emergence that are in a continual state of flux. Matter and energy—atoms, molecules, cells, organisms, light, heat, gravity, radiation—exist. Everything in existence is working itself out by natural forces that are neither designed nor intended nor morally weighted. Everything simply is. Some forces and processes generate certain outcomes; others generate others. Complex substances have slowly evolved. Life has very improbably evolved. Conscious and self-conscious human beings have even more improbably evolved.

Evolution through natural selection works through genetic mutation and selective survival. But it also involves massive death and extinction. Most of the living species that ever inhabited Planet Earth, including various protohuman groups, are now vanished. In the future many other living entities will go extinct. Through very bad natural or humanmade disasters, humanity could suffer waves of massive death and maybe near or actual extinction in the not-too-distant future.[7] Eventually, sooner or later, one way or another, all life on earth will be extinguished. And energy, matter, and natural forces will simply continue to play themselves out indefinitely.

In the meantime, lo and behold, one species, human beings, has by odd chance developed cognitive, emotional, and volitional capacities that result in their making valuations and judgments of a moral character. By "moral" here, following Charles Taylor, I mean understandings about what is right and wrong, good and bad, worthy and unworthy, just and unjust that are believed to be established not by people's own actual desires, decisions, or preferences but by sources believed to exist apart from them, providing standards by which people's own desires, decisions, and preferences can themselves be judged.[8] Viruses, ticks, and foxes do not create and live in moral worlds. But human beings, it so happens, do.[9]

Furthermore, the potential range of human moral perceptions, categories, valuations, and judgments is immense. That humans are morally *oriented* animals per se does not itself specify the *content* of human morality. In fact, within very broad functional boundaries, humans can believe, have believed, and sometimes do believe in an immense variety of different kinds of moral worldviews and commitments. There is no one single moral system that is hardwired into humanity. Humans are not naturally or automatically humanistic liberal Democrats, for example, or slave-trading racists. They have to become such things through socialization by other people and social institutions that believe in and maintain such moral systems. The recurrent existential human question, therefore, is what *ought* we to rightly believe morally? What *is* true with respect to morality? What kind of institutions *should* we promote and defend?

If we are able to slough off the superstitions and errors of premodern mythologies about spirits and gods and heaven and hell, what honest, cogent answer might we give to this perennial moral question? What might we be warranted in believing is right and wrong, good and bad, worthy and unworthy for homo sapiens scratching out an existence on the skin of this tiny planet spiraling around in an empty and inherently purposeless cosmos? Would that call for a moral commitment to universal benevolence and human rights? I am afraid, as far as I can see, that it would not.

To begin with, let us first observe that a naturalistic universe does not seem to offer any moral guidance at all. The heavens, contrary to what the ancient Psalmist wrote, do not declare the glory of God. Things just are what they are. More specifically, evolution provides no moral orientation whatsoever. For many years evolutionists believed that they could squeeze the doctrine of Progress out of evolution. But it did not take long to realize that evolution is simply an account of change, not progress or advance. Organisms do tend to "want" to survive. But on evolutionary grounds per se we cannot say that it was *morally* good or bad that the dinosaurs lived or died, for instance. It simply happened.

And if humanity were to be extinguished by a global plague, survived only by bacteria, that too would, on evolutionary terms, be morally neither right nor wrong. It simply would be what happened. The last dying humans might regret and grieve it, but in a naturalistic universe that would not make the fact immoral. The fact would simply be that some bacteria could survive and humans could not.[10] So, assuming naturalism, if morality is to be acquired at all, it must be acquired from the human mind, not from a naturalistic universe. Moral "facts" and values are simply not natural givens existing "out there" for humans to recognize and embrace. They are, rather, human constructions that people must invent, believe, more or less live by, and enforce among each other.

SURVIVAL MORALITY?

This brings us back to the question: Which moral beliefs ought contemporary and future humans to create, believe in, and live by, and why? Is there a defensible way to defeat the claims of the previous paragraph? Might the nearly universal drive of organisms to *survive* provide a clue? Perhaps, but it is not clear what that clue actually suggests. It might help if we could posit a normative "species solidarity rule" stating that each organism ought to be committed to the survival of its own species. That at least might give us a fixed starting point from which to build out an evolution-based morality. Unfortunately, using such a rule would rely on a preexisting moral obligation in order to explain the existence of moral obligations. We would then have to explain: Where did that rule come from and why ought any member of a species believe and act on it?

In fact there are human persons who believe that humans are the doom of the world and should relinquish their planetary dominance for the sake of the survival of other animal and plant species. If they are morally wrong in this, is it because they have violated the species solidarity rule? Alternatively, one might say that such a "rule" is not actually normative but merely descriptive, that members of species in fact just do happen to be "committed" to the survival of their species—and this may perhaps provide the basis of moral reasoning. But that is wrong too. Members of some animal species fight and destroy each other. Members of some species endanger themselves to protect the lives of members of other species. Are dolphins tending toward evolutionary immorality when they save swimming humans from sharks? Is a trained St. Bernard, when it saves humans buried in avalanches? Are humans evolutionarily immoral in diverting resources that could help save the lives of vulnerable humans in order to instead save animals on the endangered species list? I do not think so. This hardly seems to me a promising approach to explaining universal benevolence and human rights.

But let us try harder to derive morality from survival. Let us posit that for humans "the moral" is that which facilitates human survival. It is moral to care for the sick because doing so fosters human survival. It is moral to share one's food with the hungry because that increases the likelihood of human persistence. Et cetera. The question then is: Whose survival? The survival of an individual? A nuclear family? A kinship group? A tribe? An ethnic group? A "nation"? A "race"? The entire human species? Which and why exactly? If the subject of survival is the individual organism and its family or kin, then it is not clear why universal benevolence should be a moral fact and obligation. Individuals, clans, and tribes can simply take care of themselves and rightly be indifferent to the suffering or survival of others of their species who are just as likely to be competitors as cooperators.

If on the other hand the moral subject of survival is the human species, then it is not clear why *universal* human rights should be a moral fact and obligation. In many cases, humanity as an animal species would be much better off and could potentially evolve higher levels of reproductive fitness if our most deformed, diseased, stupid, disabled, criminal, incorrigibly unproductive, and otherwise functionally useless and defective members were eliminated. What within the parameters of naturalistic evolution exactly would be wrong with eugenics, for instance, is not all that rationally clear under these terms. Such ideas may cause revulsion in us. But my argument is simply that naturalism cannot well explain the rational justification of that revulsion.

Back to the question of deriving morality from survival and the problem of specifying whose survival. Natural selection as a process operates through the survival and deaths of individual organisms. Neither saber-tooth tigers nor manta rays ever joined in solidarity together to enhance their species' reproductive fitness. They often simply survived and died as individual organisms subject to the purposeless forces of nature. If anything, they often competed with one another for individual survival. If individuals managed to survive, then the species survived. If individuals did not, then the species did not. So which human moral system might be derived from the drive to survive? It depends again on *whose* survival.

Some advocates of "evolutionary ethics" do attempt to derive ethics from the drive toward species survival. Some in particular point to the fact of the evolution of *cooperation*. We know that some animal species, especially humans, have evolved the capacities to cooperate to achieve shared goods that enhance survival. Think, for example, of wolves hunting in packs to kill prey together that they could not kill individually, or human neighbors collaborating to raise a barn. This shows that survival is not always the accomplishment of individual organisms, even if it often is. So might the fact of evolutionarily learned cooperation serve humans as the basis for their moral commitment to universal benevolence and human rights?

I think not. The two are qualitatively different in crucial ways. Social cooperation is *situationally conditional*, for instance, while universal benevolence and rights are *categorically absolute*. Social cooperation is generated and explained *functionally* by its rewarding practical consequences; benevolence and rights of the sort in question here, however, are warranted on *principled* grounds, apart from any function or consequences. Social cooperation serves as a means for *clearly bounded* (usually small) groups of animals to enhance their reproductive fitness in the face of the dangers or pressures of other threatening animals or natural conditions; but the universal benevolence and human rights in question here are, well, *universal* in their scope, demanding moral obligation to care for and be just even to others who may diminish rather than enhance one's own flourishing. In short, evolutionarily learned social cooperation enables people under the right conditions to behave in highly "prosocial" ways. But without importing additional normative assumptions alien to naturalism, deriving warranted universal benevolence and human rights from the empirical fact of learned cooperation seems no more possible than pulling a rabbit out of a magician's empty hat.

I can imagine some saying "yes, but the time has come to extend our cooperative capacities to the entire human race. We must learn global cooperation if we as humans are to survive." As an empirical fact, that may be so (or it may not be—it is an empirical question). But even if it is empirically true, still left unexplained in the claim are the reasons justifying the words "entire" in the first sentence and "must" in the second sentence. Once again, this claim presupposes what we actually need to explain and vindicate, namely, the warranted moral force of a universalistic obligation. What if the hard *empirical* fact is actually that the human race would improve its chances of surviving if it eliminated its most destructive, unproductive, and uncooperative members? Should we maintain our commitment to universal benevolence and human rights? If so, exactly why? In the end, the sheer drive of life to survive, even given the reality of learned human cooperation, does not seem capable of providing a defensible warrant for a moral commitment to universal benevolence and human rights.

About here in this discussion, someone usually points out that human beings are dramatically unlike other species on the earth, in that we possess not only bodies capable of physical survival but also brains capable of complex forms of reasoning, anticipation, creativity, forethought, imagination, and planning. This, they say, is precisely where morality comes into play. Humans are not merely struggling to survive on the earth. They are also able to perceive and reflect on the earth's general history and condition, explain to themselves the causes and consequences of events, forecast alternative futures dependent upon different conditions, and make real choices that have consequences. Such superior cognitive capacities conjoin with sophisticated emotional and volitional abilities to generate moral categories, valuations, judgments, and action.

Fine. All of this is true. But how does it necessarily lead to the humanistic morality of universal benevolence and human rights? Such complex human capacities could just as easily lead to a warrior ethic of tribal or national conquest and dominance. To derive the kind of universal humanistic morality that many embrace today from the sheer facts of complex human cognitive capacities requires demonstrating a consistent functional benefit that such a morality provides to reproductive fitness. But universal benevolence and human rights simply do not demonstrably provide such a benefit. With natural selection, even aided by the complex capacities of human cognitive ability, reproductive fitness is most evidently enhanced when individuals seek their own material advantage and that of their families, kin, and tribes—that is, their local "in-group," those on whom their safety, security, health, and future depend. Interactions with others beyond one's in-group might advisedly be peaceful and friendly, but for strategic instrumental reasons, not because of any universal morality.

Nothing about the human capacity for complex reasoning, forethought, or planning per se naturally leads to universal benevolence and belief in human rights. It can lead to planning and cooperation, but those are a far cry from universal benevolence and human rights. The quest for survival, no matter how well aided by the powers of the human brain, simply cannot rationally get us to a genuine belief in the moral obligation of universal benevolence and the existence of inalienable human rights. Something else seems required to produce those—if not a transcendent God, then some other account or explanation.

Some at this juncture may venture the apparently reasonable idea that *globalization* changes everything. The idea is that, before globalization, when time and space greatly separated people on earth and most of the consequences of their actions from each other, an ethic of universalistic benevolence and human rights was irrelevant to survival. (Remember, survival is the sole value at present driving this argument.) However, in the globalized world in which we now live, given the huge military and environmental challenges humanity now faces, the very survival of our species depends not only on human cooperation but also on the imperative of universal benevolence and rights.

I do not see why or how this is necessarily so. What is clear, it seems to me, is that, given our global challenges, and the fact that today what some people do anywhere on earth can affect other people elsewhere on earth, the coordination and cooperation of those people with good intentions can indeed increase the survival chances of the human species. But that does not justify the more ambitious commitment to universal benevolence and human rights. If one *begins* with a moral commitment to the survival and well-being of *all* human persons, then one might explain why benevolence toward others ought to be *universal* and not selective. But, once again, that moral commitment is exactly what we are trying to explain and justify as a conclusion here. We cannot simply drop it into our thinking as an unexplained axiomatic presupposition and expect it to work.

Lacking that moral commitment to universalism as a basic premise, and proceeding with intellectual honesty in a naturalistic cosmos, I do not know how rationally to defeat certain arguments against universal benevolence and rights. I can well imagine a contrarian arguing, for instance, that in our dangerous, globalized world, we actually can no longer afford to believe in the myth of universal human rights and must prepare ourselves to eliminate those parts of humanity who most threaten the survival of our species. Such an argument would have to show that our attempting to protect and defend the existence, well-being, and "rights" of all individual humans on earth in fact endangers the overall survival chances of our species. That does not seem to me an impossible or even difficult argument to make.

Of course most modern people would consider such an argument barbaric and heartless. But the legitimate grounds for having that emotional response and making that moral judgment are precisely what we are trying to establish here and defend against skeptics. Those grounds must in the end be explained, not simply arbitrarily presupposed or emotively vented.[11] They require a cogent justification running in the background, capable of being brought to the foreground and vindicated when necessary. In the future of our dangerous, globalizing world, those wanting to continue to champion and defend universal benevolence and human rights will have to think more clearly and explain more persuasively than their skeptics, however barbaric and heartless their skeptics may seem now.

Once again, at issue is not general human survival considered in the abstract but exactly *whose* survival and on what grounds, which returns us to the problems of the "species solidarity rule." Human survival on a globalized planet in a naturalistic cosmos does seem to warrant a *practical* commitment to benevolence extended and rights granted to those others whose enhanced well-being may possibly have the effect of enhancing our own well-being and that of others we care about. But it remains unclear why such a reality justifies a genuinely *moral* commitment to benevolence and rights for all humans everywhere, no matter how their behaviors may affect one's own well-being. So once again, naturalism, even in a globalized world, seems to leave us without an adequate justification for the moral commitment that we seek to validate here. Globalization certainly raises the stakes, but by itself it does nothing to vindicate the moral imperative of universal benevolence and human rights.

Another possibility that might work if its premise was actually true would be to posit that humans possess a natural, innate sympathy for most or all other humans simply by virtue of their humanity. Adam Smith made a move like this in *The Theory of Moral Sentiments.*[12] Unfortunately, the preponderance of evidence falsifies the premise, at least the version of it that would be required to build on it a robust commitment to universal benevolence and rights. History and experience show that while people may often feel sympathy for other people, those feelings are also very often overwhelmed by the all-too-familiar forces of self-interest, insecurity, rivalry, greed, enmity, and revenge. It seems to be just as easy and likely for one to become estranged from and even hostile toward others who are different as it is to care for them and seek their good—if not easier and more likely. The power of innate sympathy is often feeble compared to other less kindly human capacities.

But *even if* natural sympathy were a common, overpowering human impulse, that itself would not establish the objective fact of inalienable human rights and moral obligations of universal benevolence. Again, widespread subjective feelings simply do not and cannot give rise to moral facts and obligations. To get from one to the other requires the recognition of an objective fact of rights and obligations whose independent existence our feelings might only suggest. For our widespread moral belief in universal benevolence and human rights does not oblige us to act in response only if and when we feel sympathy toward others. The commitment requires that we act regardless of how we may feel. In fact, the belief itself claims the authority to change how we actually *do* feel to more closely align with how we ought to feel. The moral fact of universal rights itself calls us to learn emotional responses in respect of those existent rights of others. So theories of "natural sympathies" just do not get us to universal benevolence and rights.

A SOCIAL CONTRACT ACCOUNT?

An alternative way to account for the moral obligations of benevolence and rights is to posit some sort of social contract that creates and implements them. The idea is that the moral facts and duties involved in universal benevolence and human rights are not independent realities derived from God, natural law, or any other transcendent source, to which humans respond or conform. Rather, universal benevolence and rights are ultimately human historical and cultural inventions that social collectives so happen for their own reasons to have decided to agree to define, embrace, and enforce. And by the power of a Durkheimian "conscience collective,"[13] they have come to appear to subsequent generations to have an independent, transcendent, even sacred character calling for obedience.

This social contract account may well be descriptively correct. It certainly comports with a naturalistic universe. But such an account also gives up most of the ground needed to sustain a belief in universal benevolence and rights, by shifting these from moral facts and imperatives to contingent human agreements. The vulnerability is that if a commitment to rights and benevolence is understood as merely the outcome of a social agreement, two consequences follow. First, little prevents individuals who come to believe this from selectively violating the agreement if it serves their advantage and they can get away with it (Hume's "sensible knave" again, as examined in chapter 1). Second, nothing prevents the members of any given society from deciding that they want to rewrite the social contract in ways that jettison rights and benevolence. Nothing larger could or arguably even should constrain individual "moral free riders" or collective social contract rewriters.

If benevolence and rights are ultimately only institutionalized historical constructions, then they can be individually circumvented when possible or collectively deconstructed if social circumstances seem to merit such a revision. Why should the sensibilities and agreements of generations long dead necessarily govern our lives and those who live in the future, unless it is clear how and why universal benevolence and rights serve our and their real interests? In this way, the social contract account opens the door for universal rights and benevolence to join belief in a flat earth and the divine right of kings in the dustbin of history, if contingent social conditions and events were to lead people to make that move.

Furthermore, if social contract is indeed the real source of our belief in rights and benevolence, then the enlightened few who understand this fact are also inevitably led to a position that contradicts every known principle, instinct, and experience about moral education that humans have ever had: namely that greater and better moral education does not foster more moral living. If the morality of rights and benevolence, which people normally act upon because they believe they are real moral facts and obligations, are really only historically agreed-upon human constructions, then it would be better for moral educators to hide this truth from the masses and perpetuate the contract by allowing people to think that morality is more than mere contract. It would be better intentionally to mislead and keep people in the dark in order to get them to act "morally." And that is a very strange if not perverse position in which to be.

But, again, all of this simply avoids answering the basic moral question: What *ought* human persons to rightly believe is morally true? For the social contract account is not a normative defense of the validity of benevolence and rights but a descriptive explanation for their existence and social power. The social contract account works in a naturalistic universe precisely by shifting the question away from what is normatively real and true to how empirically we came to believe what we believe. Whether or not the contract story adequately answers its own descriptive question about empirical sources, it does not and cannot compel people to believe in benevolence and rights as *moral truths* upon which they are obliged to act even if to their own detriment. That would require the more basic premise that whatever humans collectively decide becomes moral truth by virtue only of those decisions. But exactly why that should be so is unclear and remains vulnerable to the problem of moral free riders and collective social contract rewriters discussed above.

Morality of the sort we are trying to justify here has to do with what is right and wrong, good and bad, et cetera, which are believed to be established not by humans' own actual desires, decisions, or preferences but by sources believed to exist apart from them. The social contract account simply redefines benevolence and rights to be not matters of morality but of social convention. If and when people come to see these "morals" as mere social conventions, the main thing that will then compel their conformity in action is the threat of greater harm for not conforming. And that is not a prescription for sustaining a robust culture of universal benevolence and human rights.

NATURALISM'S MORALITY

Before further interrogating what I think are failed attempts to derive and defend a serious moral commitment to universal benevolence and human rights from a universe defined by naturalism, I wish to spell out an alternative moral vision that seems justifiable given the parameters of naturalism. Suppose we could completely eliminate from our minds and practices the enduring cultural and institutional influences of the Jewish and Christian metaphysics and moral orders that naturalism tells us are groundless. Suppose we could also eliminate the other culturally humanistic traditions, such as Enlightenment humanism, that have been at least indirectly dependent on transcendent or theistic metaphysics and moralities. If we could thus "start from scratch" in a naturalistic universe, not confused by superstitions and errors, and if we could exercise complete intellectual honesty in considering the moral beliefs and commitments that would be fitting for and reasonably defensible in a naturalistic universe, what kind of morality might we come up with? What moral order would make sense, given naturalism's picture of reality?

Well, one is hard pressed to come up with an answer, because it is not clear that in a naturalistic universe there *are* normative sources that exist apart from people. Matter and energy are not a moral source. They just exist and do what they do. The natural processes that govern the operation of the cosmos are not moral sources. They are simply the givens of physics and mathematics, elemental facts of natural reality lacking inherent meaning or purpose or normativity. Positive and negative electrical charges do not attract one another because that is right or just, they do so simply because that is simply how they work. The evolutionary development of substances and life forms is not a moral source. These also just happen as they happen. What then in naturalism's cosmos could serve for humans as a genuine moral guide or standard, having a source apart from human desires, decisions, and preferences and thus capable of judging and transforming the latter? I cannot think of any.

Some may claim that human morality should at the very minimum conform to the basic direction and mechanisms of physics and evolution. That, at least, would bring some consistency to the entire matter. What such a claim leaves unexplained, however, is where the "should" in that sentence came from. Why should humans conform in this way? Why shouldn't humans who are endowed with complex cognitive, emotional, and volitional powers do whatever they want to do? Why should not the "should" of such a naturalistic morality just as well be that every existent entity is free to be and do whatever it is able and wants to be and do? Molecules are and should be molecules to their full extent without unnatural normative constraints, even when they conglomerate massively and smash into and destroy other material entities. Jellyfish should be jellyfish to their full capacities without unnatural moral constraints, even when they sting, kill, and consume other living sea creatures. And humans should simply be humans to their full capabilities without unnatural moral constraints, even if this means acting out in any way whatever one's ideas, feelings, and desires make one capable of. The *ought* would simply be seeking consistency with the *is* and its capacities. What would be wrong with that?

Still, others will continue to insist—despite the discussion around survival above—that what we know about evolution does provide us with some moral parameters, even if we cannot think of evolutionary change as advance or progress. This is arguable. But let us consider it and see where it takes us. What moral direction might our knowledge about naturalistic evolution provide to us? The central moral maxim that such an approach would seem to offer would be something like this: *Each organism should do whatever it can and needs to do to survive and thrive.* (Again, it is not clear where the "should" in that sentence comes from, but let's set that issue aside for a moment.) If reproductive fitness is enhanced by engaging in cooperative social life, then that is good; if reproductive fitness is enhanced by antisocial selfishness, than that is good too. If survival is facilitated by care for the sick and weak, then that is right; but if survival is aided by leaving the sick to die, then that is right. Whatever organisms can do to survive and thrive is good, right, true, and just. This may be the closest to what we might devise as a consistent evolutionary ethic. Obviously, however, it accomplishes nothing by way of securing the moral commitment to universal benevolence and human rights.

Another approach is to ask what exactly, in a naturalistic universe, would be morally wrong with actions and practices that would violate most ordinary contemporary people's sense of benevolence and rights. Can naturalism provide coherent reasons for rejecting them? Consider, for instance, the following proposals, all of which would arguably enhance in various ways the reproductive fitness of humanity as a species.

- Cities and municipalities should be authorized to round up all inveterate drug addicts, incorrigible drunks, and long-term homeless people and either deploy them in socially beneficial projects of forced labor or euthanize them. Such people are socially unproductive, destructive, and hopeless and have forfeited their "right" to life and liberty.
- Babies who are born with incapacitating physical or mental defects should be allowed to die—their parents can try again to have healthy babies to replace them. Parents, especially in societies with high population pressures, who give birth to healthy but unwanted babies should also be allowed to let them die. Better to have societies populated by wanted and well-cared-for children.
- All elderly persons who have finished their productive and reproductive decades and are now living out their last years as dependent invalids in expensive hospitals and "assisted

living" facilities should be removed from social and medical support and allowed to die. This policy would particularly apply to the suffering, terminally ill, and those whose life
savings or family members cannot cover the cost of their care.
Half of all medical costs today are said to be spent on people's
last six months of life. Why? Let the dying die. Use those resources for more productive purposes.

- All persons convicted of serious criminal offenses, especially
  multiple offenses and multiple convictions, should, if they are
  allowed to live, be involuntarily sterilized so that they do not
  pass on their potentially criminal genetic material to future
  generations.

- Long-term patients in mental hospitals and insane asylums
  who show no promise of recovery from their serious illnesses
  should be euthanized.

- Penal systems should return to more punitive arrangements
  and practices to not only serve as expensive protec-
  tive holding tanks for criminals but to proactively punish
  criminals for their offenses, as a means to raise the costs of
  crime and so perhaps to deter other prospective criminals
  from wrongdoing.

Of course, such suggestions violate the moral sensibilities and
commitments of most contemporary readers. But that is primarily
because most readers are the heirs of millennia of cultural moral
traditions rooted in transcendent monotheism that gave compelling accounts of universal human dignity and destiny that unfolded
historically in complex ways and that now demand universal benevolence and respect for human rights.

But what if the naturalist worldview is true? What if those
cultural traditions were built on error? What if transcendent

monotheism turns out to be a myth? What if our actual human situation is one of accidental species existence lived out in cosmic solitude on this minor planet rotating away toward eventual oblivion in an inherently purposeless, meaningless, and standardless cosmos that operates according to impersonal and uncaring physical forces? Does it matter then that demented old people are allowed to die now instead of a few years later? Is it "wrong" to forcibly bar criminals from having children? Would it be an injustice to allow a severely mentally disabled baby to die, hopefully to be replaced by another healthy baby? If so, on what grounds? By what standard? Why does it matter morally? Who in the long run would know or care or enforce any consequence?

In a naturalistic universe, everyone would not have to become savages or cunning egoists. Any given person might be free to simply choose to want to be a caring, self-sacrificing humanist. A naturalistic morality could afford people such a choice. But, again, such a commitment must also accept the status of an arbitrary, subjective, personal preference. No account could be given within the bounds of naturalism as to why such a commitment is preferable or ought to be binding on others. If other people wished instead to embrace full-scale eugenics and a ruthless survival-of-the-fittest culture, that would be legitimate and defensible as well. Lacking a moral standard truly external to human ideas, feelings, and desires by which those ideas, feelings, and desires could be judged, it is not clear why we would not have to accept most every expression of human thought, affect, and will as morally licit. What else would humans have upon which to construct being and action?

Moreover, in a naturalistic universe, those smarter, stronger, more attractive and charismatic people with the capacity by force or deception to foist their ideas, feelings, and desires on others would be entitled to do so. Perhaps they might even compel others to embrace and internalize their own preferred moral views and practices, so that others would come to believe that these views and practices were universally good, right, true, and just. Why not? Those who can, will. (In fact, it seems to me a matter of fact that for the most part today, those who can, actually do.) In the end, however, a widespread belief that those moral views were true and universal would not make them so. At bottom, they would simply be some dominant people's imposition of their arbitrary views on other more compliant people.

In short, naturalism, when taken with all seriousness and honesty, would most likely liquidate our standard concept of morality. "Morality" itself—as involving standards external to our own thoughts, emotions, and desires—would have to dissolve or transmute into some other different thing. Even if we provisionally allow ourselves to smuggle into our considerations a normative "should" that actually seems alien to naturalism, the moral orientation we then derive is oriented to practical functionality and unequal merit in human survival and reproductive fitness. Universal benevolence and human rights are still nowhere near explained or secured. And if we resort to free human choice for belief in benevolence and rights, in doing so we redefine them as arbitrary subjective preferences holding no more inherent authority or attraction than an alternative commitment to warrior conquest and glory, pitiless strategic egoism, sadism, or utter relativistic nihilism. They are all equally legitimate potential personal inclinations.

OTHER DEFICIENT ACCOUNTS

All of this is nuts, some readers may be saying by now. Moral philosophy has produced numerous rational ethical systems that do not appeal to transcendent metaphysics yet point to the truth and goodness of benevolence and rights. I wish that this were so. It is true that moral philosophy has generated such moral systems, but philosophy has also just as effectively pinpointed their intellectual faults and failures. All versions of such rational, nontranscendent moral philosophies, it turns out, fail to account successfully for universal benevolence and rights in one or both of two ways. Either they surreptitiously smuggle in assumptions and commitments from the Judeo-Christian or some other moral heritage, or they simply fail on their own terms as rational systems justifying universal benevolence and rights. I have already discussed such problems with the social contract account above. Here I briefly examine a few other possibilities.

Utilitarian moral reasoning at first appears compatible with a naturalistic universe, as it appeals only in its moral calculations to human pains and pleasures, defining the moral good as that which produces the greatest happiness for the greatest number. Doesn't utilitarianism as a philosophy focused on human happiness offer us a moral system capable of underwriting universal benevolence and human rights? Well, no, actually. For one thing, utilitarianism is incapable on its own terms of explaining why anyone *should* actually be committed to the happiness of the greatest number. Why not—given utilitarianism's assumption of hedonic individualism— simply be concerned with one's own pleasure and happiness and perhaps those of the other people we care about? If we humans are simply biological bundles of phenomenally experienced pain and pleasure that constitute happiness and unhappiness, why be obliged to maximize *general* happiness?

Motivating utilitarian calculations to that end requires a prior moral commitment to maximal collective human happiness—a commitment that utilitarianism itself cannot produce or justify.

Furthermore, even if we grant the maximum collective happiness premise, utilitarianism is oblivious to inalienable human rights. In fact, if feeding members of a minority religious group to lions for the stadium entertainment of the masses would increase the overall, calculated, bottom-line happiness of the collective, then doing so would be moral in utilitarian terms—the increased happiness of the masses would outweigh the lost happiness of those fed to the lions. In the end, since pleasure and happiness are simply on a qualitatively different plane than innate, universal human rights, utilitarianism is unable to get us from the former to the latter. If anything, utilitarianism greatly endangers the latter, as we see, for example, in the writings of the Princeton utilitarian ethicist Peter Singer, who suggests allowing babies born with defects to die so they may be replaced with healthy siblings.[14]

What about Kantian ethics? Well, Immanuel Kant actually *did* appeal to a transcendent reality to make his ethical approach work. While he critiqued traditional proofs of God's existence, in most of his other work across his career Kant maintained that the very possibility of "the Highest Good" for humans is dependent upon the postulates of the existence of an omnipotent, omniscient, and just divinity and an afterlife and some kind of immortality of the human soul.[15] Nonetheless, some contemporary Kantians, including explicitly atheist moral philosophers, wish to adopt Kant's general approach to ethics minus any transcendent reference. Does that work? Kant did not think so. But let's see.

Kant's categorical imperative teaches that we should *"act so as to treat humanity, whether in your own person or in others, always as an end, and never merely as a means,"* in order that we may fulfill the general formula of the moral law, namely, *"act so that the maxim may be capable of becoming a universal law for all rational beings."* Surely this rationally explains why all persons ought to respect and respond to the obligations of universal benevolence and human rights? Unfortunately, not really, at least not again without first smuggling in a prior moral commitment not itself derived or justified by a secular version of Kantian ethics.

The main problem with the atheist's use of Kant's ethic for our purposes here, as Alasdair MacIntyre has shown in *After Virtue*, is its failure to finally explain why anyone ought to be committed to following it in the first place.[16] Kant's system may work well as a moral guide for the person *who is already committed for other reasons to* universal benevolence, fairness, justice, kindness, and so on and is looking for a handy rule by which to make specific moral decisions. Such was the case for Kant himself, who came to his philosophical work having already absorbed and taken for granted the moral commitments and sensibilities of his own pietistic Lutheran cultural upbringing; and who, again, explicitly appealed to transcendence as a kind of "moral backstop." Kant never doubted what the content of a good moral life looked like. What Kant's moral philosophy provided was something like concise rules for judging rationally whether one's specific moral choices were correct and would fit what he took to be legitimate moral commitments—judgments that did not have to appeal directly to God or the Bible.

But minus a transcendent reference, Kant's moral system does not provide an account of why anyone ought to be bound to following those moral commitments to begin with. Suppose that you are inclined toward serious rational egoism and not benevolence. In that case, the right thing for you to want is actually not to treat all other people as ends and not means. Rather, the correct thing for you to want is for everyone else to treat you as an end, but for you to be free selectively to treat other people as means if and when that serves your self-interest—which often it clearly can and does (Hume's sensible knave yet again).[17]

Kant therefore may be helpful to those who are already committed to living a moral life characterized by respect, duty, reasonableness, and munificence. But for people who are living in a world without divinity and a universe without larger meaning or purpose and are looking for a good and compelling reason to believe in universal benevolence and human rights, the Kantian approach minus transcendence comes up short. Against many disagreeable alternative moral viewpoints, what a secular Kantian can say in riposte is that they violate respect for reason and good will—hardly a vigorous argument against such rivals, who simply counter: "Who gives a damn? To hell with your good will." In short, secular Kantians *presume* respect for reason and good will rather than rationally justifying and necessitating them. The naturalist challenge requires a better account than Kant minus transcendence can give.

Some may protest here that my objections to these standard moral philosophies presuppose some pretty antisocial people not willing simply to go along with benevolence and respect for others' rights. Yes, quite right, that is precisely the point. It turns out that in the world we live in there are plenty of such people around. Moreover, there are antisocial capacities, if not propensities, in nearly all people, myself included. Neither an attitude of optimism nor "Up with People" rallies will be enough to address the moral challenge. If universal benevolence and human rights as moral facts and imperatives are to be sustained in this world, that will require credible explanations and accounts that legitimize practices and institutions sufficiently compelling to override the parochialism, selfishness, and enmity that real existing humans are so very capable of generating among themselves and against each other. "All you need is love" and "Everybody get together" turn out to be very big orders. The question, then, is what metaphysically or otherwise grounded morality can generate such love and solidarity in a world so pathetically lacking in love and solidarity? I am afraid that neither the utilitarian followers of Jeremy Bentham and John Stuart Mill nor secular Kantians have the answer.

Finally, let us consider the position of "self-evident moral realism," of which the work of the University of Wisconsin moral philosopher Russ Shafer-Landau is a good example.[18] Shafer-Landau rejects moral relativism and defends objective moral realism, not by appeal to a divinity or transcendent command but by arguing that moral principles simply exist. They just are. Moral facts are part of the furniture of our reality just by virtue of the way it is. Moral truths make up the distinctly moral world that we find ourselves inhabiting, simply as it is, just as the laws of physics and chemistry describe what is true about aspects of the material world that they address. People don't invent these moral principles, nor do they necessarily derive from the will or character of God. They simply are what they are, just part of the fabric of our reality.

Shafer-Landau writes: "we are not the authors of morality, but rather are constrained by moral rules not of our own making. . . . Moral principles and facts are objective in a quite strong sense: they are true and exist independently of what any human being, no matter his or her perspective, thinks of them."[19] And again: "if some [moral] standard is true, irreducibly, and to be construed realistically, then nothing *makes* it true; its truth is not a creation, but instead a brute fact about the way the world works."[20] Furthermore, for any reasonable and properly formed person, moral truths will be self-evident. By that Shafer-Landau means that "adequately understanding and attentively considering just [a moral proposition] is sufficient to justify believing that [moral proposition]."[21] Included in the list of moral propositions Shafer Landau believes are self evident are the propositions that, other things being equal, "it is wrong to take pleasure in another's pain, to taunt and threaten the vulnerable, to prosecute and punish those known to be innocent, and to sell another's secrets solely for personal gain."[22]

What might we say about such an argument for our inquiry here? Doing justice to his sophisticated argument is well beyond the scope of these few paragraphs. For present purposes, suffice it to say that *if* Shafer-Landau's self-evident moral realism is correct, then naturalism as I have described it here is in big trouble. Shafer-Landau asserts the real self-existence of moral principles and facts possessing genuine normative authority. And these are not reducible to matter and energy and whatever else constitutes "only nature," as naturalists understand it. Indeed, Shafer-Landau's moral theory is explicitly *anti*naturalist. We need, he argues, to "introduce into our ontology a *sui generis* category of values. . . . I think moral facts are different in kind from any other [facts]. We should resist the naturalist's pressure to see all reality in terms amenable to scientific confirmation. What is needed, then, is a defence of ethical *non-naturalism*."[23] But, he claims, "the best scientific views will not reveal the existence of moral properties, because moral properties are not scientific ones. Doing ethics is not doing any kind of science. Therefore there is a class of things (moral properties) that exist in addition to the battery of things that science can reveal to us."[24]

Once that move is granted, naturalism unravels.[25] Self-evident ethical nonnaturalism complicates reality in ways naturalism cannot handle. "Non-naturalism's ontology cannot be as compact as that of . . . classical naturalism," Shafer-Landau says. "There are (at least) two kinds of properties, and therefore (at least) two kinds of facts."[26] One involves natural facts, and the other involves sui generis moral facts, which cannot be reduced to natural facts. Furthermore, "at least some fundamental moral truths are knowable a priori," that is, without the need for scientific investigation.[27] And in resisting the claims of naturalism, Shafer-Landau says, "non-naturalists have nothing to be ashamed of with their relatively expansive ontology."[28]

Shafer-Landau thereby opens up space for immaterial, nonnaturalistic features of reality, one of which is moral facts. His ethics thus require "a kind of metaphysical pluralism, one that allows for more than one kind of property and fact in the universe."[29] But having opened the door to the existence of immaterial moral principles and facts, let us note, there is no obvious reason why something like a natural law or cosmic forces like karma, for instance, should be automatically ruled out of bounds. They need not be ruled *in* bounds—they are not required—but nothing in principle in Shafer-Landau's ethics must or can exclude them either, as far as I can see. The same is true about the possible existence of an immaterial divine being. Shafer-Landau is not closed to these possibilities, even if his defense of moral realism does not depend upon them. He expressly states: "I want to remain neutral here on theological matters."[30] And his position, quoted above, that "there are (at least) two kinds of properties, and therefore (at least) two kinds of facts," obviously implies that there could possibly be three (or more) kinds of properties and facts belonging to reality (perhaps including ones that would invalidate atheism).[31] At bottom, then, if Shafer-Landau's argument and others like his are convincing, then metaphysical naturalism is rejected.

But for argument's sake, let us loosen up the parameters of our analysis. Let us set aside the concern with naturalism and focus instead on atheism. Let us suppose that a version of Shafer-Landau's case is correct in which in reality only two (and no more) kinds of properties and facts exist: (1) scientifically discoverable natural facts, and (2) self-evident ethical facts having no religious basis. That is, no divine, transcendent, or (quasi-)religious property like karma exists, even though moral facts exist. We would then have a version of Shafer-Landau's self-evident moral realism that a nonnaturalist atheist could embrace, by accepting the reality of immaterial, non-natural moral facts while still rejecting the existence of God or other religious entity related to those moral facts. Does that secure us universal benevolence and human rights?

The answer is: not now and probably not ever. Shafer-Landau has not listed universal benevolence and human rights among the moral facts he believes are self-evident, and I doubt he would ever attempt it.[32] Let us be clear: a vast distance separates "do not inflict pain on others for your own pleasure" from "actively practice benevolence toward and champion the human rights of all people everywhere, as you are able." The first is prohibitive and narrow, the second is proscriptive and globally expansive, among other differences. Of course, an atheist moralist may assert that universal benevolence and human rights are part of the self-evident moral furniture of reality. But to be persuasive on Shafer-Landau's terms, the atheist moralists need their claim to pass the *self-evident* test. Given all I have argued above, we have little reason to expect to see that happening.[33] The doubts of the moral skeptics are sure to prevail on this point, and reasonably so. In any case, as it currently stands, the burden rests with those who think otherwise. And until that is accomplished, I stand by my case that a naturalistic universe—even a "modified" one that admits immaterial, nonnaturalistic entities— does not rationally justify a commitment to universal benevolence and human rights.

BUT CAN WE SUSTAIN IT ANYWAY?

Here I would like to return to address the third question posed at the outset: *If* my answer to the second question as argued above is correct—that intellectual honesty does not grant residents of a naturalistic universe warranted moral belief in universal benevolence and human rights—will human societies and cultures who want to believe in them anyway, for whatever reasons, be able, notwithstanding the lack of warrant, to sustain such beliefs over the long run? I think the answer to this is arguable.

On the one hand human cultures demonstrate amazing capacities to carry on institutional practices long after their animating sources have withered. Max Weber's book *The Protestant Ethic and the Spirit of Capitalism*, for instance, illustrates how the sixteenth- and seventeenth-century Protestant Reformation's "worldly asceticism" gave rise to theological and spiritual categories and practices that arguably helped foster the emergence of modern capitalism, which has since continued as the world's most powerful social institution despite the decline of doctrines about predestination, salvation, and hell. Weber may be mistaken on some of his historical details, but the larger theoretical point still holds—cultural ideals and practices often survive the environments that produced them, can transpose into novel parallel forms, and frequently have long shelf lives. Perhaps belief in universal benevolence and human rights has taken on a cultural life of its own, apart from the transcendent metaphysics that helped give birth to it, and will be able to carry on through inertia into the human future indefinitely.

At the same time, sociological understanding also suggests that beliefs and ideas require institutional resources to sustain them. Values, categories, norms, and viewpoints do not operate like perpetual motion machines. Entropy is always at work. Alternative values, categories, norms, and viewpoints are always competing for adherents. In order for belief commitments—especially challenging and costly commitments—to endure over time and space, they must benefit from institutionalized resources and customs to reinforce and validate them. Resources are scarce and tend to gravitate to compelling ideas and opportunities to generate more resources. Time and again, in the historical record of cultural change, beliefs and values once prized have come to seem outmoded, irrelevant, passé, not worthy of allegiance.

We cannot predict whether this would happen to the now widely accepted modern belief in universal benevolence and human rights if and when increasing numbers of people come to grasp and internalize the full meaning of life in naturalism's universe. But if my argument above is valid and if our common belief in benevolence and rights were to gradually or suddenly slip away, that would, in my view, be a tragedy of unspeakable proportions. I shudder to think of my grandchildren and their children and beyond having to live in such a world. For this reason, I suggest that it is worth our reconsidering the necessary metaphysical and cultural bases of the moral facts and obligation to which we are committed, now, while they are still understood and practiced, even if for flimsy reasons.

CONCLUSION

Let me be clear about the claims here. My argument has not demonstrated that we do not live in a naturalistic universe. We may. My argument only concerns the reasonable consequences for our ideas about universal benevolence and human rights if that is the case. Neither has my argument established the truth of transcendent monotheism. That was not the point. My more limited claim on that matter is simply that transcendent monotheism was a crucial condition in giving rise historically and culturally to our current commitments to benevolence and rights.

Furthermore, I am obviously not suggesting that only Judaism and Christianity foster people's acting morally. Certain significant standards of substantive morality—against unjust killing, lying, stealing, and so on—are (contra strong cultural relativists) found in and supported by every human culture. Rather, I am speaking more precisely to the much higher standard of morality demanded by universal benevolence and human rights. Belief in these is not in fact universal—although many moderns would like it to become so—and therefore needs explaining and defending.

Let us suppose then that we are interested in sustaining and strengthening the modern moral commitments to universal benevolence and human rights. Let us say that we want on moral grounds everywhere to eliminate slavery, child abuse, political imprisonment and torture, the sex trade, and the like. Let us agree that we ought to live in a world in which people and nations do what they can to stop disease epidemics, aid the victims of catastrophe, and oppose the gross exploitation of the poor, no matter where and to whom these happen. And let us suppose that it is not only perhaps situationally beneficial but also truly morally good for people to be interpersonally kind, thoughtful, and fair to other people. The question is: What kind of reasoned basis and moral culture do we need to vindicate those commitments and practices?

The condition for these having evolved into existence in the first place was the historical emergence of transcendent monotheism, first in Judaism and later continued by Christianity. The question we now face, I suggest, is whether the metaphysical worldview of naturalism that has in many quarters displaced transcendent monotheism as the predominantly authorized view of reality can provide the intellectual and emotional foundation to sustain this belief in benevolence and rights. I know there are smart people who think it can. But I simply cannot see, for reasons explained above, how that is so. And so I fear that in the naturalistic universe that atheists promote, universal benevolence and human rights will in due time as cultural objects go the way of the dinosaur. And that would be an unfortunate unintended consequence of the triumph of atheism, and the metaphysically naturalistic view that is its partner, if they indeed triumph.

We may hope that I am wrong. But hope itself is not enough. What we also need is an articulation of some rational and compelling account for high moral standards of benevolence and rights—if indeed such an account exists. Nothing short of this is needed for the sake of our children, grandchildren, and all future generations whom we want to live in humanistic, not inhumane societies. Meanwhile, until that articulation is accomplished, atheists ought, I suggest, to consider the possibility that they are indeed overreaching in their claim to be able rationally to justify a commitment to universal benevolence and human rights.

Chapter 3

Why Scientists Playing
Amateur Atheology Fail

In this chapter I address a specific concern related to the very big topic of the proper relation of science and religion.[1] This is a hugely important issue, one that has generated a lot of controversy. The topic is important because science and religion are both weighty matters in their own right, because science and religion address questions and make claims about some of the same subjects, and because how we think science and religion ought properly to relate to each other has big consequences for how we think about life and how we operate important social institutions such as schools. There is a lot of misguided and sloppy thinking about science and religion going on these days, including among some otherwise very smart people, and critiquing that can help to sharpen our own critical thinking skills. The question also touches on some key claims made by numerous contemporary atheists.

I am a sociologist who is also interested in certain philosophical questions. So I am going to engage some philosophical issues here, but in a way that is framed by a sociological perspective. Arguments about science and religion concern not only clear and unclear thinking about ideas, which philosophy encourages us to grapple with, but also the question of the control of *turf*. By "turf" I mean something like the areas of neighborhoods ruled by gangs. With science and religion, the turf in question is not controlled by threats and violence but by institutionalized beliefs about authority and legitimacy that are struggled for and carefully protected by groups of people with divergent interests. The *general* sociological question is: Who has the right, the competence, the legitimate authority to make claims that stick, claims that others should recognize as valid? The specific question here is: What kinds of issues and claims is *science* legitimately authorized to address and make? And what kinds is *religion* legitimately authorized to address and make? This is a *sociological* issue because it concerns the cultural construction of claims-making authority by different and sometimes rival social groups and institutions.[2] I will complicate this turf metaphor in a bit, but it is a good place to start.

I have observed that certain well-known science authors, often writing for popular audiences, seem to feel entitled not only to write with authority about science but also to pronounce on metaphysics and religion. And I think that is often a problem.

Here is what I mean. I read a lot of books about science. I really believe in the importance of science and want to learn from science all I can. I don't mean that I read supertechnical science books but those written for the well-educated public. What I have noticed in reading such books is that their authors sometimes abruptly slip from making scientific claims based on scientific methods and evidence to asserting metaphysical and theological claims, seemingly based on scientific authority but in fact having no properly scientific merit. These statements are often non sequiturs. Invariably, they contradict and dismiss religion. Most are made by professed atheists. They are clearly meant to undercut religious claims, authority, and plausibility.

Here is one example. Recently, I was reading the globally bestselling 2015 book *Sapiens: A Brief History of Humankind,* by the Oxford-educated Israeli scholar Yuval Noah Harari.[3] In it, Harari pulls together massive amounts of scientific evidence to tell us about the long story of human biological and cultural evolution. His references are empirical, reasonable, and mostly impressive. So I was enjoying this book when, on page 28, I suddenly found myself reading these words: "there are no gods in the universe . . . outside of the common imagination of human beings." "No . . . things [like gods] exist outside of the stories that people invent and tell one another." "Religious myths" are "imagined," "fictions" produced from "collective imagination," not *"objective* reality." I found these claims really jarring. I had just been reading Harari's story about the human Cognitive Revolution, which good empirical evidence demonstrates occurred many tens of thousands of years ago. Next thing I know and without warning, I'm reading *theological metaphysics:* "There are no gods in the universe." Really?

How, I wondered, does or could Harari possibly know these things? From artifacts dug up in archeological excavations? From fossils archived in natural history museums? I think not. Said plainly, Harari is here engaging in a deceptive sleight of hand, an unacknowledged smuggling of atheological metaphysics in through the back door of science, ostensibly with the authority of science. I have no doubt that Harari would on principle defy religion's setting two toes onto science's turf. But he obviously feels entitled to wander onto religion's turf, to pour a tank of gasoline on it and to set it on fire. Worse, he does not even seem to be aware of his own intellectual category-shifting here.

I will provide other examples like this hereafter, but first I want to make a crucial distinction. That is between (1) a scientist publicly offering a *personal* confession of his best evaluation of all of the available evidence and concluding that *he* cannot as an individual believe certain religious claims, and (2) a scientist publicly suggesting or claiming with *scientific* authority that what science has learned itself shows that religious claims are false or almost certainly false. The first position is legitimate. All scientists have the right to decide for themselves whether they can or cannot believe certain religious claims, and the findings of science may certainly play an appropriate role in that discernment. Furthermore, scientists, like everyone else, have the right to tell others about their personal beliefs. It is the second case that I take issue with. Scientists as public intellectuals have no legitimate intellectual grounds for many of the dismissive metaphysical or religious claims they make, supposedly on the basis of the findings of science.

Just to make sure you do not think I am cherry-picking an anomalous passage from an exceptional case, let me offer other examples of atheist scientists interloping in this way onto the turf of metaphysics and theology. In a book published in 2014, the biologist Edward O. Wilson claims: "the evidence is massive enough and clear enough to tell us this much: We were created not by a supernatural intelligence but by chance and necessity. . . . There is no evidence of . . . [a] demonstrable destiny or purpose assigned to us, no second life vouchsafed us for the end of the present one. We are . . . completely alone."[4] Really? Empirical evidence tells us that? How so?

The University of Hawaii particle physicist, Victor Stenger, similarly writes: "empirical data and the theories that successfully describe those data indicate that the universe did not come about as a purposeful creation. Based on our best current scientific knowledge, we conclude beyond a reasonable doubt that a God who is the highly intelligent and powerful supernatural creator of the physical universe does not exist."[5]

Paleoanthropologist Richard Leakey and science writer Roger Lewin claim that the "important message that comes to us from the fossil record" is that any (alleged) "God surely had no plans for *Homo sapiens*, and could not even have predicted that such a species would ever arise."[6] For a final example sufficient for present purposes, Marcelo Gleiser, a Brazilian physicist and astronomer on the faculty at Dartmouth College, writes: "there is no Final Truth to be discovered, no grand plan behind creation."[7]

In case you think this kind of writing is only a recent expression of the New Atheism, think again. It has a long history. Consider, for example, this statement from Bertrand Russell, the British mathematician, logician, and philosopher, published in a 1903 article in the *Independent Review*, which describes "the world which Science [capital S] presents for our belief":

> Man is the product of causes which had no provision of the end they were achieving. . . . His origin, his growth, his hopes and fear, his loves and his beliefs are but the outcome of accidental collections of atoms. . . . No fire, no heroism, no intensity of thought and feeling can preserve an individual life beyond the grave. . . . All of the labors of the ages, all the devotion, all the inspirations, all the noonday brightness of human genius, are destined to extinction in the vast death of the solar system. . . . The whole temple of man's achievements must inevitably be buried beneath the debris of a universe in ruins—all of these things . . . are so nearly certain that no philosophy which rejects them can hope to stand.[8]

So "Science" here is supposedly telling us what we must believe about the meaning and purpose and destiny of humanity and the universe: namely, there is none.

Really? Science can tell us that? No, it can't. The "meta" prefix of "metaphysics" makes a huge difference in distinguishing it from mere physics. So does the "theo" prefix in "theology" make it a fundamentally different discipline of inquiry from other "ologies" like biology or cosmology.

Yet scientists regularly venture such claims anyway. Consider this more recent statement by the physicist Steven Weinberg in his book *The First Three Minutes*:

> It is almost irresistible [although false] for humans to believe that we have some special relation to the universe, that human life is not just a more-or-less farcical outcome of a chain of accidents reaching back to the first three minutes, but that we were somehow built in from the beginning. . . . It is very hard to realize that this is all just a tiny part of an overwhelmingly hostile universe. It is even harder to realize that this present universe has evolved from an unspeakably unfamiliar early condition, and faces a future extinction of endless cold or intolerable heat. The more the universe seems comprehensible, the more it also seems pointless.[9]

Weinberg here is trying to drive us from a physics description of the Big Bang, about which he has real expertise, to the conclusion that the universe is in fact pointless, which his expertise does not authorize him to make. What entitles him to move from science to metaphysics so effortlessly? It's unclear. And my simple point here is that it is illegitimate. The metaphysics does not rationally follow from the science, and never could.

So on what grounds do such scientists seem to think they are entitled to pronounce like this on metaphysics and theology, when they are not philosophers and theologians? Some, I suspect, do not even realize what they are doing. They appear simply to be oblivious to the relevant epistemological and discursive boundaries and so do not realize that they have wandered onto someone else's turf. The simple word for that, I am afraid, is "ignorance." Others, it seems, appear simply to believe that because they speak with the authority of science, they are authorized to pronounce authoritatively on any topic. The simple word for that is "arrogance." It goes without saying that neither ignorance nor arrogance befit good science, or those who represent science to the public.

However, what I observe in such science writing is not simply the result of ignorance and arrogance but instead also often follows from a particular assumption that is powerful but rarely explicitly stated. This assumption is fallacious. It sounds like this: if science cannot observe or discover something, then it cannot be real or true. Stated slightly differently: the only things that could be true or real are those that science can observe and validate. This is what we call vulgar imperialistic scientism. (Not science but the ideology of scientism.) And running at even deeper levels, driving imperialistic scientism, are the prescientific presuppositions of naturalism, materialism, and empiricism. With all of these assumptions at work, science is turned from (1) one fantastic way to know many things about ourselves and the world into (2) an imperialistic, exclusivist, totalizing source of any and all legitimate knowledge about everything. All comers must enter by the narrow gate of The Scientific Method if they hope to be welcomed into the Kingdom of Knowledge. This very scientism is clearly reflected in the passages by Wilson, Stenger, Leakey, and Lewin quoted here, which try to make "empirical data," "massive and clear evidence," and "the fossil record" the sole adjudicators of God's existence and a purpose for the universe.

To spell this out a bit further, let's return to Steven Weinberg's claims about the universe being pointless to see how this works.

He has repeated his view about the pointlessness of the universe in other places. In one of them, he tellingly says: "there is no point in the universe that we discover by the methods of science. . . . [We are] faced with this unloving, impersonal universe [and] *we* make [in it any that there is] warmth and love . . . for ourselves."[10]

I do not disagree with Weinberg's first statement, that "there is no point in the universe that we discover by the methods of science." Of course physics cannot discover a point to the universe any more than my kitchen thermometer could tell me what emotions you are feeling inside. Weinberg's statement about what science cannot discover is obvious. But the problem is that he concludes that because science cannot discover it, there actually in fact is no point to the universe. That is silly. Simply because physics cannot discover the universe's possible point does not mean there isn't one. All that Weinberg's conclusion really tells us is that he comes to his argument operating with the working presupposition of imperialistic scientism, that is, that if science cannot observe or discover something, then it cannot be real or true. If we reject that presupposition, as we should, then by other means the universe might be found to have a point, a meaning, a significance.

The bemusing irony in all of this is that the presupposition that authorizes only science to tell us what is real and true, and that produces such dramatic conclusions about the universe's pointlessness, is not itself a scientific statement and could never, ever itself be validated by empirical science. It is instead a philosophical presupposition, something not unlike a faith commitment. The logic of imperialistic scientism, then, turns out to be internally self-defeating. It depends on a nonscientific position to take the position that only science authorizes us to take positions worth taking. And that is like calling someone on the telephone to tell her that you cannot call her to talk because your telephone is not working. The very claim itself shows that the claim cannot be correct.

A second irony here is that, in the name of hard-nosed intellectual rigor, many such public-intellectual scientists show themselves to be deeply confused about the basic nature of the religious ideas they dismiss. For instance, the God of the Abrahamic traditions of Judaism, Christianity, and Islam is by nature radically transcendent, of an absolutely different order of being from creation, and so of course is not subjectable to human empirical observation and experimentation. Any even half-educated believer in these traditions knows that God cannot be subject to human empirical observation and experimentation. So such scientists are essentially saying to religious people: "I am going to ignore your religion's *actual* claims, which I am sure are dumb, and instead substitute my own caricature of them; then I am going to dismiss my ill-informed caricature as failing to pass the test of my scientific standards, and then conclude that your religion is not believable." This we are supposed to take as a model of intellectual rigor?

I rather think it is an embarrassment, of exactly the sort noted by the British Marxist Roman Catholic literary critic Terry Eagleton, whose *London Review of Books* review of Richard Dawkins's book *The God Delusion* begins thus:

> Imagine someone holding forth on biology whose only knowledge of the subject is the *Book of British Birds*, and you have a rough idea of what it feels like to read Richard Dawkins on theology. Card-carrying rationalists like Dawkins . . . are in one sense the least well-equipped to understand what they castigate, since they don't believe there is anything there to be understood, or at least anything worth understanding. This is why they invariably come up with vulgar caricatures of religious

faith that would make a first-year theology student wince. The more they detest religion, the more ill-informed their criticisms of it tend to be. If they were asked to pass judgment on phenomenology or the geopolitics of South Asia, they would no doubt bone up on the question as assiduously as they could. When it comes to theology, however, any shoddy old travesty will pass muster.[11]

Now, to be very clear, I am not saying that no religious claims could be disproved by science, that all religious claims are somehow protected from scientific scrutiny simply by virtue of being religious. No, in fact any religious claims that concern workings in this observable world are potentially liable to scientific invalidation—if and when science has the tools and evidence to evaluate them. If, for example, a faith healer claimed to have cured someone's cancer but medical tests showed the cancer remaining, the faith healer's claim would be invalidated. If science could figure out a way to send researchers back through a time machine to observe the few days after Jesus's crucifixion and made a video recording of the disciples stealing Jesus's dead body from the tomb and then claiming that Jesus had risen from the dead by the power of God, that would put an end to all but the most demythologized liberal Christianity. Or if historians with new empirical evidence were somehow able to show beyond a reasonable doubt that the claims of Joseph Smith about the revelations of the golden plates in the woods in upstate New York were a hoax, that would sink Mormonism. Usually the passage of time and the lack of evidence (or time machines) make such scientific invalidations of religious claims impossible, for better or worse, even if in principle they would be possible. But my main point here is a conceptual one: some religious claims about reality are in principle subject to scientific evaluation, and some—those inherently beyond science's capacity to observe and analyze—simply are not.

Now back to sociology. The fact that the kind of science writers I have quoted blithely interlope in metaphysics and theology without compunction and sometimes, it seems, even without awareness that they are doing it, and that they usually get away with it reflects not only ignorance and arrogance and scientistic ideology but also the institutional fact that science has accumulated massive cultural authority, status, and prestige in the public sphere, much more than religion possesses. And, however much modern people, including scientists, would like to believe that we operate purely rationally, we know that cultural status cognitively biases people's tendency to offer and accept beliefs generally, even erroneous beliefs.

Put differently: science is a dominant institution when it comes to knowledge claims. And one of the privileges of dominance is not having to learn and think as hard as one should when it comes to making claims beyond one's core competence. Peripheral voices, by comparison, have got to think very hard about their claims if they hope not to be dismissed as sectarian but instead to have their ideas taken seriously by the mainstream. But when one is already, by virtue of one's great institutional status and authority, Taken Very Seriously, one can afford to get a bit intellectually sloppy with one's claims and still get away with them.

Once all of these institutional forces get moving in the same direction, the kind of public representatives of science I have quoted can take advantage of and reinforce the following double standard:

1. On the one hand the religion of religious believers is a *personal* matter that must as subjective opinion be kept closeted

in private life, and certainly not be allowed to say anything about science or education.

2. On the other hand in the hands of scientists, religion is a *public* matter subject to reductionistic dismissals on the authority of supposedly objective science.

In other words, viewed as turf struggles between science and religion, the science gang has gained nearly complete control of the religion turf. Members of the religion gang may stay in their neighborhood, as long as they keep off the streets. Then again, for representatives of the more aggressive, New Atheist persuasion—like Dawkins—the religion gang needs simply to surrender and disappear.

Let us set this question of turf struggles in some historical context. The institution of Western science has spent the last few centuries working to establish its autonomy from religion, magic, hucksters, superstition, and other cultural entities that it sees as making competing and erroneous claims about how the world works. That is, science has struggled against perceived rivals—such as young-earth creationists and defenders of intelligent design—to define a controlled turf of knowledge-claims over which it has authorized, professional, institutional jurisdiction. And while, like most such struggles, this has involved some unfortunate and embarrassing episodes—such as, for example, mainstream science's authorization of the eugenics movement prior to World War II—I think, personally, as a believer in science, that this has largely been a good and legitimate process.

And as part of that process, science has increasingly insisted that—whether or not religion is a good and valid thing in and of itself—religion should not try to make claims that do not belong within the limits of its proper epistemological jurisdiction. Science's authority to tell us that we live in a heliocentric solar system, for example, ought not to be questioned by the possible religious claim, based on misused scriptural evidence, that we live in a geocentric solar system. (Here I refer to the Galileo affair, an incident that looms large in the minds of most of science's boundary police.)

Now, assuming that it is a fair demand of science that religion should not intrude on science's legitimate turf, I think it follows that science, given its inherent limitations, should also not intrude on religion's legitimate turf when it lacks the competence to make claims about metaphysical theology, as it almost always does. At the very least, when science writers publicly pronounce on metaphysics and theology, they should be obliged to satisfy two conditions. First, they should learn enough about real metaphysics and religion to be able to speak accurately and intelligently about them. And second, they should make clear in their writing and speaking that they are no longer making *scientific* claims but rather switching modes of discourse and epistemological frameworks to discuss metaphysics or religion. To fail to do either of these I think is irresponsible and deceptive.

But to be clear, we must observe that the situation here is more complicated than science and religion simply needing to respect each other's turf, because the metaphor of turf and gangs implies equal kinds of rivals fighting with the same sorts of weapons over control of territory. In fact, that is exactly how the misguided writers I quote above seem to view reality, which enables them to think that science can simply vanquish religion as a competitor. However, my most important point here is that science and religion or meta-physics are actually not equal rivals struggling with the same means over identical turf. Instead they operate on different axes of thought according to distinctive epistemological sources and standards.

So whether or not certain religious claims are actually true or false, it is inherently beyond the scope of the proper competence of science to address and judge most of them. Thus, when Harari argues that "according to the science of biology, people were not 'created.' They have evolved," he not only wrongly thinks that evolution and creation are mutually exclusive but also fallaciously assumes that biology is somehow actually equipped to disprove the existence of a creator God.[12] What is most fundamentally wrong about the science writers I cite above, in other words, is not that they are disrespecting a "rival gang's turf" but that they are making a basic category error in thinking in the first place that they can even judge such religious claims with scientific tools.

Now, to be perfectly clear, I am *not* saying that science "owns" "the facts" and religion is stuck with a crazy "leap of faith." That simple dichotomy is false too. Science is itself grounded on a set of presuppositions that are ultimately taken on faith or not. And, as Michael Polanyi has shown, scientific discovery is actually driven not by strict adherence to some Method but by deeply personal, prescientific commitments to human values like wonder, beauty, and truth. Both science and religion are thus implicated in personal belief commitments of various kinds, and to the evaluation of the truth of those beliefs through the facts of lived experience. These processes are not identical, but neither are they absolutely different. However, the difference that *does* matter here is something like this: science seeks to understand the natural workings of matter, energy, life, the mind, and society that can be theoretically understood through direct and indirect empirical observation, whereas most religions seek to understand and engage either realities that transcend creation, even if they interact with creation, such as a personal God (as in Abrahamic faiths), or realities that the immanent material world actually obscures, such as the force of Brahman (as in some forms of Hinduism and Buddhism). In both cases, even the most powerful of science's tools are constitutionally incompetent to penetrate and evaluate religion's claims. These may be humanly known, but if so it must be through means other than scientific experiment, such as divine revelation or enlightenment, operating with reason and experience.

One last thought about explaining scientists smuggling metaphysical atheology into their science writing. I think when we get down to it, a good part of what motivates many of these scientists to reject God, religion, and other nonnaturalistic metaphysical views are not really the findings of science but instead personal moral and emotional objections. I do not wish to psychoanalyze atheists. But many years of discussions and observation have suggested to me that in many cases, if one scratches just below the surface of many allegedly scientific objections to religion, one finds not scientific problems but instead often very personal moral and emotional concerns. These may be understandable, valid, and compelling. But let us be clear that they are not science. Some science writers are more transparent than others. Consider, for example, Steven Weinberg again, who in a 2003 interview said:

> Maybe at the very bottom of it. . . . I really don't like God. You know, it's silly to say I don't like God because I don't believe in God, but in the same sense that I don't like Iago . . . or any of the other villains of literature, the god of traditional Judaism and Christianity and Islam seems to me a terrible character. He's a god who [is] obsessed [with] the degree to which people worship him and anxious to punish with the most awful torments those who don't worship him in the right way. The traditional God [is] a terrible character. I don't like him.[13]

Or take Edward O. Wilson's moral objection to religion: that "faith is the one thing that makes otherwise good people do bad things. . . .

The great religions are . . . tragically sources of ceaseless and un-necessary suffering. They are impediments to the grasp of reality needed to solve most social problems in the real world."[14] Again, we can understand these personal moral and emotional objections to religion (even if they are grossly overstated). But they are not good science, or indeed science at all, and ought not to carry the weight of scientific authority, even if those who personally feel such moral objections and emotions are scientists professionally.

Before I finish, let me clarify two points. First, nothing I have said here validates the truth claims of any religion. That is not my point. All I have said is that science, by virtue of the inherent limits of what science is and does, cannot validate (or for that matter re-fute) atheism, a pointless universe, a nihilistic destruction of all things human at the end of time, or any similar claim of metaphys-ical atheology. And so scientists should not suggest otherwise. At best, science can help to fill out a picture of the world and universe we live in that contributes to our discerning judgments about the plausibility of religious truth claims. And different people in good faith can and do end up making different judgments about religion, both believing and unbelieving. The fact that scientific evidence underdetermines that outcome does not make anything about reli-gion true. That is a separate question.

Second, it must be said that not all popular science writers play at amateur metaphysics and theology. Some, such as the Johns Hopkins University neuroscientist David Linden, are quite thoughtful and careful in their views; Linden writes, for example, that "although the details of particular religious texts are falsifiable, the core tenets of many religions . . . are not. Science *cannot prove or disprove* the cen-tral ideas underlying most religious thought. When scientists claim to invalidate these core tenets of religious faith without the evidence to do so, they do a disservice to both science and religion."[15] Other writers, although they are clearly antireligious, are also more careful in the way they state their critiques. Such authors usually do clearly throw the authoritative weight of science behind the idea that religion should go the way of the dinosaur. But at least they do so more carefully, suggestively and not categorically, leaving open slight possibilities that religious claims might actually have some truth or value. Such more careful writers may actually be sociologically more dangerous to religion, but intellectually we should respect their more appropriate precision in presenting their views.

Here then is my bottom line. To all amateur scientific interlopers into metaphysics and theology, I say this: stop overreaching. Please stick to what you are good at, to science proper, and stop doing half-baked philosophy and theology without even being clear that this is what you are doing. At the very least, learn enough to be able to distinguish between properly scientific, philosophical, and theological claims. Then, if you really want to make public claims about metaphysics and theology, first learn enough about the philosophy and religion you are engaging to speak accurately and intelligently about them, so as not to embarrass yourself. And while you are at it, please think harder about the presuppositions of naturalism, materialism, and empiricism that drive you into narrow imperialistic scientism. They are seriously problematic. Hopefully you will then realize that science qua science is constitutionally incapable of disproving the possible reality of what is most important in most religions: whether that be the God of Abraham, Saint Paul, Muhammad, or Zoroaster *or* karma, samsara, reincarnation, or nirvana. Let's have good, rigorous arguments about science and religion. But let's have ones that are well-informed, fruitfully constructive when possible, and fair and honest when they must be critically destructive.

Chapter 4

Are Humans Naturally Religious?

Are human beings somehow naturally religious?[1] Should we take religion to be in some way an innate, instinctive, or inevitable aspect of human consciousness, experience, and life? Or is religion a nonessential, historically contingent aspect of human being? Various thinkers in different places in history and life have offered different answers to these questions without coming to agreement. I hope here to answer them in a way that incorporates some previous thinking yet moves toward a more realistic and helpful understanding. My answer to these questions is shaped by the philosophy of critical realism, which I think helps us do better social science than other options, especially positivist empiricism and postmodern deconstructionism. Is it possible that people and societies could become thoroughly secular, as many atheists hope? Or is that just "not in the cards" of human nature?

These are not merely issues of academic curiosity. The truth about religion and human being carries big implications for how our personal and social life should be properly ordered. Some answers to the questions imply positions about the truth value of religious and secular claims about reality. Answers and arguments about them are also bound up with massive alternative historical projects that seek to shape social orders today and into the future—by this

I mean everything from movements for secular modernism to religious theocracies. These include the Enlightenment project of a rational, secular modernity and various religious projects to build a modernity that socially accommodates, if it does not center, religious worldviews. The futures of some civilizations around the globe are today being contested by movements that are underpinned by different answers to the questions posed above. Many atheists today are pushing hard to eliminate religion from human life.

The stakes are high for implications in public policy, institutional practices, and deep cultural formation over time. Not surprisingly, many of the players in the discussions, including academics, have personal, ideological, moral, and emotional investments in the issues at hand. However, as we participate in the shared project of (from a critical realist perspective, at least) seeking to know what is true about what is real, we must let the best available evidence and best thinking about it determine our conclusions, not what we wish or hope to be true because of personal ideological or theological commitments.

FRAMING THE QUESTION

It is impossible to understand current debates without knowing something of the history of their emergence during the breakdown of Western Christendom over the last 500 years. I commend Brad Gregory's book *The Unintended Reformation: How a Religious Revolution Secularized Society,* which provides an illuminating background for my discussion.[2]

Suffice it to say for present purposes that both the Catholic Church and the Protestant reformers assumed and argued that God had planted in all humans an innate capacity and desire to know, love, and serve God—a capacity that, however, had been more or less marred by the effects of sin. So in the West there is a long theological history to these questions, which over time have been transposed into social science and philosophy debates. Notions of "human nature" in the West cannot be understood apart from their background in Christian theology's discussions of humans' orientation to God, sin, human sociability, moral virtues, and so on. The skeptical Enlightenment's project—to reconstitute social order on rational, secular, scientific grounds rather than on the basis of religion—not only polemicized against religion but forcefully denied that religion was an essential or ineradicable aspect of human nature.[3] These views helped establish some of the deep cultural assumptions underlying this discussion today. The academic study of religion (itself in part a product of secular modernity reconfiguring academic departments of theology) has been split on the question of religion and human nature. Many influential older scholars (such as Rudolf Otto, William James, and Mircea Eliade) argued, in a quasi-liberal Protestant mode, that an awareness of and magnetic attraction to "the holy," "the numinous," "the sacred," "ultimate concerns," and so on was native to human consciousness, thus locating the naturalness of religion in human subjective experience.[4] More recently, other theorists—postcolonial and postmodern— have argued that "religion" as an entity actually does not exist beyond the relatively recent, contingent constructions of Western modernity, thus calling into question the very idea of "religion" and essentially dissolving the discipline's subject of study.[5] (I find neither of these approaches persuasive, even if they contribute some useful ideas and perspectives.)[6]

Some sociologists of religion, such as Andrew Greeley, Daniel Bell, Rodney Stark, Robert Bellah, and Don Miller, have suggested variously that humans are inherently "unsecular"; that only religion answers well the most profound of humanity's existential questions and is therefore an ineliminable feature of human cultures; that humans wish for benefits that can only be obtained through exchanges with supernatural beings believed to exist in otherworldly contexts; that humans have an innate yearning for ecstasy and transcendence; and so on.[7] On the other hand different theorists—including Bryan Wilson, Steve Bruce, the early Peter Berger, Pippa Norris and Ronald Inglehart, and Phil Zuckerman—imply or argue that religion is the contingent product of certain historical and social conditions that can, may, or do dramatically diminish and perhaps ultimately disappear when social conditions change under the conditions of modernity.[8]

THE EVIDENCE

So what ought we to think? The empirical data tell us four facts. First, very many individual people in the world are nonreligious, and certain entire cultures appear to be quite secular, without immediate apparent damage to human happiness or functionality. Not all people and societies are religious or apparently have to be in order to remain contented and functional. That suggests that religion is in some sense not natural to human being but an accidental or inessential aspect characterizing only some humans.

Second, religion generally is not fading away in the modern world as a whole;[9] and even the most determined attempts by powerful states to repress and extinguish religion (e.g., in Russia, China, revolutionary France, etc.) have been less than entirely successful.[10] In addition to appearing to be primordial in human history,[11] as well as present in one form or another in all civilizations, religion thus also seems to be incredibly resilient, incapable perhaps of being destroyed or terminated. That suggests that religion is in some sense irrepressibly natural to human being.

Third, even when traditionally religious forms of human life seem to fade, new and alternative forms of life often seem to appear in their places that also engage the sacred, the spiritual, the transcendent, the liturgical, the implicitly religious, and the ecstatic. Many observers have noted, not incorrectly I think, that a vast variety of seemingly nonreligious human activities embody and express at least quasi-religious, if not overtly spiritual, features. New Age ideas and claims to be "spiritual but not religious" are obvious cases. Scholars have also noted the religious dimensions of organizations, movements, and practices as different as "secular" environmentalism, academic economics, modern nation-states, and arena sports spectacles.[12] It is also hard to miss the presence of superhuman powers, supernatural realities, and spiritual themes in some of the most popular contemporary films, fiction, and television shows.[13] Furthermore, a *variety* of arguably religious practices—besides the typical Protestant mode of centralized belief and resulting practices—are clearly involved in even traditional religious faiths, including things like what scholars call "vicarious religion," "believing without belonging," and myriad manifestations of "everyday religion."[14] This evidence suggests (though hardly proves) that religion may be in some sense irrepressibly natural to human being.

The fourth fact worth noting is that different people and peoples can and do head in quite different directions when it comes to religion. No one narrative or trajectory tells the whole story. There may simply not be a dominant story. At best, scholars can note and interpret broad patterns and associations. But the outcome of religion in human social life is highly dependent upon the particularities of history and context. That suggests that if religion is in any way natural to human being, which is not certain, then whatever it means to be "natural" has to allow for a great deal of variability and contingency.

What should we make of these four empirical facts, which do not at first seem to produce one consistent conclusion? I believe it is possible to frame a theoretical account of religion and humanity that does justice to all of the evidence above. But getting to that account requires sorting out some basic issues first.

PROPERLY DEFINING THE ISSUES

The kind of theoretical account needed to make the best sense of the evidence will have to proceed, I am convinced, with critical realism, and not positivist empiricism, operating in the background as the guiding philosophy. Many of our problems and failures in social science result from research being framed by positivist empiricism, which asks us to suppose that social reality normally operates according to something like "covering laws" that can be expressed in this form:

if $A \to$ (probably) B (all else being equal)

Positivist empiricism tells us to look for regular associations between observable empirical events and defines "explanation" as the identification of the strongest, most significant associations between them. It also sets the expectation that once the covering laws have been identified, they will apply to all cases and situations that the laws govern—this is usually assumed, if only by default, to mean "people" generally. All of that gets researchers thinking in yes/no, either/or, correct/false terms (modified, however, by the introduction of statistical probabilities and the ceteris paribus clause). Applied to the question at hand, the debate normally proceeds on the unquestioned assumption either that humans are naturally religious (and so religion will always persist in human societies) or are not naturally religious (and so modernity may or will profoundly secularize people and society).

Critical realism reconstructs many of our basic assumptions, telling us to ask different questions, and thus opening up new, helpful possibilities of understanding and explanation. Here is not the place to explain critical realism in detail.[15] For present purposes, I want to focus on its emphasis on natural capacities, powers, limitations, tendencies, and contingencies. According to critical realism, myriad kinds of real entities exist, each of which possesses particular innate characteristics.

For our purposes here, the following points are crucial. First, real entities with essential properties exist in reality, often independent of human mental activity. Second, real entities possess certain innate capacities and powers, existing at a "deep" level of reality, that only under certain conditions are activated so as to realize their potential. This means that certain natural features of entities can be entirely real but at times inoperative and unobserved. Third, when the causal energies of entities are released in particular cases, they are neither determined nor determining, neither absolutely predictable nor random, neither chaotic nor incomprehensible.

Fourth, the social scientific task is not to discover the covering laws that explain and predict observable associations of conditions and events ("if A → [probably] B [ceteris paribus]"). The task rather is for our theorizing minds to use all available empirical evidence and powers of reason to develop conceptual models that as accurately as possible descriptively represent the real causal processes operating at a "deeper," unobservable level of reality, through the agency of real causal mechanisms that produce changes in the material and nonmaterial world (some of which) we observe empirically.

Fifth, we must always pay close attention to the environmental and contextual factors that do and do not activate the causal capacities and powers of different entities, which then produce a variety of possible, sometimes-observable outcomes. In all of this, we have to be ready to deal with major complexity.

Having sketched these few key ideas from critical realism, our next task is to define "religion." This has been a matter of ongoing and vexing dispute among scholars. I define "religion" as "a complex of culturally prescribed practices that are based on premises about the existence and nature of superhuman powers."[16] These powers may be personal or impersonal, but they are always superhuman, in the dual sense that they can do things humans cannot do and that they do not depend for their existence on human activities. Religious people engage in practices intended to gain access to and communicate or align themselves with these superhuman powers. Their primary hope in doing so, I believe, is to avert misfortune, obtain blessings, and receive deliverance from crises in this life and perhaps after death.[17] People are religious, on this view, in order to tap those superhuman powers to help them avert and solve problems they confront—from getting hurt or sick to suffering a bad existence after death. This substantive definition of religion provides traction for identifying when religion is present or absent, stronger or weaker, in human life. It does not focus on religious beliefs but on religious practices. That complicates the picture described by those, like Zuckerman, who observe that highly secularized societies are often "without God" though "not without religion."

Finally, to answer our questions well, we have to clarify what we mean by "naturally" and by "nature." It turns out that "nature" is difficult to define. I here spare the reader the details of the problems involved and simply assert that critical realism provides the most sensible way to proceed. By "nature," as related to something like "human nature," I as a realist mean the stably characteristic properties, capacities, and tendencies of human beings. Specific entities in reality are what they are and not other things. These possess certain features, causal powers, and dispositions (and not others) that adhere in their being. These properties, capacities, and tendencies inhere in the entity itself.

Everything in reality has some kind of nature, in this sense, insofar as entities possess and so can express particular characteristics, capacities, and tendencies by virtue of simply being what they are. It is in the nature of real entities to have certain features, causal powers, and dispositions that distinguish them from other entities that they are not. When such features, causal powers, and disposition are not accidental, random, or unstable characteristics of an entity, but instead typify the entity in ways that are stable and commonly shared by all entities of that type, we can refer to them as their "nature." This approach recognizes that many parts of reality are neither (entirely) humanly constructed nor readily susceptible to intentional change. Different parts of reality have different inherent features, causal powers, and dispositions by virtue of the nature of what they are. Reality itself, therefore, has a certain structure or "grain" in its features, abilities, tendencies, and operations, which one can work either with or against, with varying consequences.

A CRITICAL REALIST ACCOUNT

With the foregoing clarifications in view, I propose the following answer to the question of whether or not humans are by nature religious. I begin by stating my position negatively. First, humans are not by nature religious, if by that we mean that all human persons are driven by some natural and irrepressible need or instinct or desire to be religious. In that sense, some humans are religious, and some are not, often quite happily and functionally so, it appears. Thus, to begin, the answer is no if the question refers to a universal demand for religion operating at the level of individual persons.

Second, humans are not by nature religious, if by that we mean that every human culture has a functional need or intractable impulse to make religion a centrally defining feature of society. Societies, like individuals, vary in how important a role religion plays in their lives. Some are highly religious. Others are quite secular, with religion operating on the margins, in private or in secret, far from the institutional centers of material and legitimate-knowledge production and distribution. At most we might say that total irreligion and complete secularity appear to be impossible among humans at the societal level. But that is a long way from saying that humans are naturally religious.

That said, I do believe that human beings are naturally religious when that is understood in a particular way. All human persons are naturally religious if by that we mean that they possess a complex set of innate features, capacities, powers, limitations, and tendencies that capacitate them to be religious (i.e., to think, perceive, feel, imagine, desire, and act religiously) and that, under the right conditions (which are very common in human experience), strongly tend to predispose and direct them toward practicing and believing religion. The natural religiousness of humanity is not located in a naturally determined common pattern of empirical religious practice, on the part of individuals or societies (which is how positivist empiricism would focus our attention). It is instead located in the distinctive, inherent features, capacities, powers, limitations, and tendencies of human persons that are rooted, ultimately, in the human body and brain and the emergent (often nonmaterial) capacities that arise from the body and brain.

I am speaking here of very powerful causal forces and dispositions that are rooted in the nature of reality and are chronically triggered to become operative in human life in a variety of social contexts. That helps to explain religion's primordial, irrepressible, widespread, and seemingly inextinguishable character. It also suggests that the skeptical Enlightenment, secular humanist, and New Atheist visions for a totally secular human world are simply not realistic—they are cutting against a very strong "grain" in the structure of reality and so will fail to achieve their purpose.

But that is not the whole story. Humans being "religious by nature" in this sense does not tell us to expect the eventual "return of religion" everywhere or that people will be unable to function reasonably well in the absence of religion. Neither does it license observers to decide that nonreligious people are really "anonymous" religious believers or somehow pathological or subhuman in their lack of religiousness. Nonreligious humans, like all persons, possess the natural capacities and tendencies toward religion but, for whatever reasons, have either (1) not had those capacities and tendencies activated by environmental, experiential triggers in the first place, or (2) had them activated but subsequently neutralized or deactivated by some other experienced causal forces.

I have written at length about such natural human features, capacities, powers, limitations, and tendencies in *What Is a Person?: Understanding Humanity, Social Life, and the Good from the Person Up*.[18] For present purposes, suffice it to say that they start at the "bottom" with capacities for consciousness and unconsciousness, work upward emerging through a variety of increasingly complex and sophisticated capacities and powers, and culminate with the highest-level capacities of language, symbolization, valuation, creativity and innovation, understanding of causation, self-reflexivity, creating and communicating meanings, narration, anticipating the future, identity formation, self-transcendence, truth seeking, abstract reasoning, moral awareness, aesthetic judgment, forming virtues, and interpersonal communion and love. These natural capacities dispose humans to an immense number and variety of activities and practices.

Among them are the abilities and, when activated, tendencies to (1) conceptualize and believe in superhuman powers; (2) engage in activities designed to seek help from superhuman powers (such as prayer, worship, sacrifice, and obedience); (3) anticipate alternative futures related to the superhuman powers, dependent in part on courses of action taken regarding those powers; (4) subjectively experience communion, union, harmony with or affirmation from superhuman powers; (5) engage in social relationships that reinforce belief in the reality of the superhuman powers; (6) learn to interpret the larger world and experience in light of the beliefs associated with the superhuman powers. Crucial in all of this are the capacities for symbolization and language.[19] At the same time, those capacities run into major contradictions when they "hit the wall" of natural human limitations and constraints. Religion arises out of the dynamic tension generated by the confrontation of humans' natural capacities and limitations, where what humans can do and what we cannot do collide.

What exactly do I mean by natural tendencies toward religion? I mean the propensities caused by an interconnected set of orientations toward life and the world that humans recurrently experience. In some sense we are here speaking about "the human condition," but not one that is vaguely existentialist. The human condition I mean emerges directly from the innate features of the human body as it operates in its material and nonmaterial environment[20]—particularly from the collision between its natural powers and its natural limitations. At the same time, this human condition is not absolutely determined and determining—there is space for the consequences of the somewhat free play of human desires, emotions, and beliefs.

The first of these natural tendencies toward religion springs from our universal human epistemic condition. In the final analysis, all humans are believers generally, not knowers with certitude, with respect to what is real. This point I have argued at length in *Moral, Believing Animals: Human Personhood and Culture* and will not repeat here.[21] It is enough to say that everything we humans ever "know" is grounded on presuppositions that are the necessary conditions to get inquiry, perception, and knowledge-building off the ground. And those beliefs simply cannot be verified with proof that assures us with certainty that they are true and right. All humans are thus believers before and more basically than we are knowers.

That is as true for atheists as for religious adherents. In the end, none of us can find and build upon certain, indubitable truths that are not dependent upon more basic presupposed beliefs (what philosophers call an attempt at "foundationalist" knowledge). This quest for foundationalist certainty, with which we are likely familiar, is a distinctly modern project that was launched as a response to the instabilities and uncertainties of early modern Europe, with Descartes its pioneer. But that modern philosophical foundationalist project has failed. There is no universal, rational foundation upon which indubitably certain knowledge can be built. All human knowing is built on believing. That is the human condition. And that means that religious commitment is not fundamentally different, at bottom, from all other human belief commitments, insofar as religion involves trust in and response to believed-in realities that are not objectively verifiable or universally shared by all reasonable people. Religious believing is thus not at odds with the broad trajectory of all human believing.

And that helps to incline people, under the right conditions, toward religion.

A second feature of the human condition that gives rise to a tendency toward religion concerns the capacity to recognize and the desire to solve problems. Following my definition of religion above, we see that religion has its deepest roots in the desire to avert, forestall, and resolve real and perceived problems. Among all the animal species on this earth, humans, their lives being so very complex, are particularly likely to encounter a wide variety of material, bodily, psychological, and social problems. Humans are also particularly well capacitated to recognize problems, define them as problems, and desire to overcome them.

Finally, because humans are so very finite in their capacities, they are likely to encounter problems that they have limited or no power to solve. Human capacities to know what is happening in life often outstrip human power to control it. Very often, yawning chasms stand between people's problems and their abilities to solve them. Yet humans find it difficult to ignore their problems. When the prospect of a helpful superhuman power is present, it is quite natural for humans to be interested in the possibility of appealing to those powers to help avert or resolve their problems (unless some other stronger causal power neutralizes that interest).[22] Comparatively, the "hamster condition" and even the "chimpanzee condition" are not like that, and they are naturally not capacitated for or tending toward religion.

The human condition also lends itself to the tendency toward religious engagement. Humans recurrently ask and wrestle with what Brad Gregory has called the "Life Questions": "What should I live for and why? What should I believe and why should I believe it? What is morality and where does it come from? What kind of person should I be? What is the meaning of life, and what should

I do in order to lead a fulfilling life?"[23] Daniel Bell similarly noted a set of questions that, he argued, call humans back to religion in order to answer well, namely, "the core questions that confront all human groups in the consciousness of existence: how one meets death, the meaning of tragedy, the nature of obligation, the character of love—these are recurrent questions which are, I believe, cultural universals, to be found in all societies where men have become conscious of the finiteness of existence."[24]

Humans have both incredible capacities and severe limits, and that contradiction continually produces pressing difficulties. We have the capacity to know we will die but not to know what comes after. We tend to seek truth, goodness, and beauty but find little of it in this world and often in ourselves. We are meaning-making and significance-seeking animals, yet our ability to spin satisfying meanings solely from within the horizons of the immanent world we occupy is limited. Historically, religion has been a primary way that humans have answered these questions, and I am confident that for many people it will continue to be.

But this is also crucial to realize: religion is not the only way for humans to answer these big Life Questions and live seemingly functional, happy lives. The human condition does not require people to be religious. Indeed, not all people feel the need to address and answer such questions—many appear happy to focus on the present, live as well as they can, and not be bothered by the Big Questions, including the problem of death. At the same time, however, the capacity to respond to the human condition in terms that are not religious does not mean that that this existential condition does not exist. It does. We are dealing with causal forces that need to be activated and with tendencies, not with perfect associations or necessities. And such forces and tendencies are shaped by particular historical and social conditions and experiences.[25]

Finally, the human moral condition inescapably involves the making of "strong evaluations" (in Charles Taylor's words),[26] based on moral beliefs that we take to arise not from our personal preferences and desires but from sources transcending them. It is simply *un*natural, in the strongest sense of that word, for humans to think that morality is nothing but a charade, that even the asking of moral questions is wrong-headed, that all moral claims are nothing but relative human constructions. Friedrich Nietzsche attempted some version of this, but he could not finally escape the necessity of arguing that some things were in fact true, that some positions were actually right—which is why he wrote his powerful works to convince his readers of his views. His "transvaluation" of all values ended up committing him to certain truth claims and senses of normative good and bad. "Slave morality" was bad, for instance, while the morality of the noble warrior was good.

Humans thus find themselves having to operate with some account of where morality comes from, what makes it real. Some people are clearly able to submerge such questions below the level of consciousness. But the questions recur in cultures and social groups, if not in the lives of individual persons. Religions are not the only answer to the question of moral sources, but historically they have been foundational and central.[27] Secular modernity is arguably radically incoherent and self-deceived on matters of moral philosophy.[28] Most people are not moral philosophers, who have a professional interest in intellectual consistency, but the questions themselves never disappear. They return again and again in the course of human experience over time.[29] This, too, under the right conditions, I suggest, triggers human capacities to be disposed to religious answers and practices.

But how, critics might ask, can we distinguish genuine, natural human tendencies from any other factor that might produce one or another human activity? One way to sort this out is to consider how relatively easy or hard it is for natural human capacities to be expressed in particular ways. The harder people have to work to produce something in human life, the less likely it is that humans have a natural tendency for it. It is a natural tendency, for example, for people to use their capacity for muscle motion in their legs and arms to walk and to feed themselves, but not to crab-walk backward or repeatedly hit themselves in the head. Across human history and societies, it is possible to find a dizzying array of expressions of human potentials. But some of them are rare and difficult to achieve, while others are common and easy.

Viewed broadly (not just thinking of modern Europe), religion tends to fall into the latter category. In most historical situations, it has not been hard for people and cultures to come to believe, embrace, practice, and pass on religions to subsequent generations. It has been much, much harder to extinguish them.

In fact, it usually takes some combination of potent religion-undermining experiences, like many decades of sustained ideological attacks (as with skeptical Enlightenment polemicists), the trauma of demoralizing wars (as in the early modern so-called "wars of religion"),[30] religiously significant atrocities (such as the Holocaust), sustained internal religious conflicts (as in Europe after the Protestant Reformation), or purposive state repression (such as Soviet-enforced atheism), to suppress human religious practices. And even then the outcome is not certain. All of this tells us something: that humans not only have the capacity to be religious, like the capacity for anything else humans can do, including rare and difficult things, but also those capacities are directed by strong, natural tendencies that turn them toward religious expression. In short, humans not only have latent potential for religion but also very strong natural tendencies toward practicing religion. That contributes to my argument that, understood in a particular way, humans are naturally religious.

My argument can be summarized as follows. Simply because some feature of human being is natural, that does not mean that it always is or needs to be expressed, acted upon, or found necessary or attractive to all humans or to most humans in any particular culture. Many natural features and capacities in reality, including human reality, are not often activated. Others are activated but subsequently countered or neutralized by other factors.

We can confidently say that humans are naturally religious or by nature religious—as a matter of real, natural potential, capacity, and tendency—while at the same time acknowledging that many humans and even some cultures are not particularly religious at all.[31] Such an account entails many implications, theoretical and practical, worth considering. But it strongly suggests that we should not expect human societies to become thoroughly secularized on any long-term basis.[32] Secularization as a process will likely be limited, contingent, and susceptible to reversal. The New Atheist dream of a fundamentally secular world will prove illusory.

Conclusion

Many atheists today make bold claims about morality, science, and the naturalness of secular life. Atheists can be "good without God," they insist, just as good as, if not better than, religious people. Atheism and the metaphysically naturalistic cosmos it heralds can sustain the received humanistic heritage of universal benevolence and human rights. Atheism is the clear truth as demonstrated by the evidence of empirical science. And a secular existence is within reach of humanity if only people would leave behind the superstitions of religion. Such claims are common among atheist activists. They have to be. For if atheism is not compatible with moral excellence, universal benevolence, human rights, the authority of science, and basic human nature, then its attractiveness is significantly diminished.

I believe these atheists are overreaching in all of those claims. They are not absolutely wrong. But they are overplaying their hand, trying to claim more for their viewpoint than reason and empirical evidence justify. Such overreaching must be called out. The issues involved are too important to let such unsupportable claims stand. Atheism will not benefit in the long run by staking out strong positions that do not hold up to scrutiny.

CLAIMS AND CLARIFICATIONS

To be clear, let me restate what I am not claiming here. I am not arguing that atheism is wrong. I am not arguing that theism is right. I am not saying that atheists have no reason to behave ethically. I am not suggesting that atheism leads to moral nihilism. I am not saying that science is incompatible with atheism. I am not suggesting that all people are somehow covertly religious. And I am not saying that secular people and cultures cannot live happy, meaningful lives. Nothing I argue in this book makes or even suggests those claims.

What I have argued and concluded is this: atheists have good reasons to adhere to a modest or moderately demanding morality based on enlightened self-interest and buttressed by social compacts and the punishment of defectors. But that kind of moral standard, if it is self-reflective and intellectually honest, ought not to expect people to provide equal treatment for all other humans, but rather ought to expect people to privilege those who are socially closest to them; and it will always be vulnerable to the doubts of moral skeptics and the exploits of "sensible knaves" who ethically free ride on others who are consistently good. This I think is as much ethically as atheism can justify.

Furthermore, the naturalistic cosmos that is the standard operating worldview of atheism cannot with rational warrant justify the received humanistic belief in universal benevolence and human rights. Historically in the West, those very demanding commitments germinated in the soil of theism were later transplanted into the religiously mixed grounds of the Enlightenment, flowered in the twentieth century after World War II, and diffused culturally through a variety of nonreligious and religious movements and institutions.

Considered rationally, metaphysical naturalism is simply not a worldview that independently possesses the intellectual resources to warrant a commitment to benevolence afforded and human rights honored for all humans everywhere. If naturalism is true, therefore, the future of universal benevolence and human rights stands in jeopardy.

Moreover, contrary to some atheists' claims, science in no way demonstrates empirically or even by "inference to the best explanation" that the kind of transcendent God of the Abrahamic traditions of Judaism, Christianity, and Islam does not exist. Atheists who maintain otherwise exhibit an inexcusably misguided understanding of both science and religions. A proper reading of these matters rightly concludes that science is inherently incapable of proving or disproving God's possible existence. Overreaching atheists who are intellectually honest should moderate their claims that science empirically verifies their beliefs.

Finally, contrary to an atheist hope that human societies might readily become secular, human beings turn out to be strongly disposed to believe and practice religion. Humans are not naturally religious in the sense that religion is inevitable in human lives and social institutions. But we are naturally religious in the sense of possessing by nature not only the complex capacities but also the recurrent, strong inclinations to cognize, believe, and observe religious ideas and practices. Human societies and subcultures around the world are highly variable when it comes to religion and nonreligion. But atheists have little reason to be confident that human societies are on a path toward steadily increasing secularization. Atheist overreaching has tried in various ways to deny or ignore these realistic conclusions, which accomplishes little good for anyone.

ARISTOTLE IGNORED

The first half of this book is about the ethical possibilities available to atheism. While working through atheists' arguments for being "good without God," I was surprised and baffled by their near total lack of interest in Aristotle. The atheists I read wanted to provide a sound basis for ethical living in a universe absent a transcendent divinity. To this end they continually relied upon various amalgamations of social contract theory, Kantian rationalism, and utilitarianism, often bolstered by generous helpings of undue optimism. I have attempted to show that their efforts do not succeed, at least in justifying what I called a strong or high standard of morality. While working through their arguments, however, I kept wondering why they never turned to Aristotle for help. Aristotle seems very well suited for their task.

What does Aristotle offer atheist ethics? To be sure, like Kant, Aristotle cannot be imported directly into atheism, since he, like Kant, developed his ethics against the backdrop of a belief in the existence of God.[1] Even so, Aristotle's ethics can, I think, be adjusted and deployed in an atheist universe—and more persuasively, I believe, than the alternatives.[2]

Aristotelian virtue ethics reference the universal human desire to realize the rewards of a good life well lived (*eudaimonia*). The ultimate motive to learn and practice the virtues is to achieve what is by nature inherently and inescapably good for all humans: their own thriving and happiness. The problem of providing reasonable moral skeptics and sensible knaves a justified motivation to observe in practice the moral good, even when it is costly, is thus eliminated. The atheist activists I examined could never on Kantian, utilitarian, and social-contract grounds adequately solve that motivation problem. Aristotle solves it for them.

Furthermore, Aristotle's ethics are not unrealistically demanding or naïvely optimistic. They never lead us down the path of wishful thinking about human goodness, onto which some atheist writers wander. Aristotelian ethics do not expect people to become shining angels or selfless altruists. It instructs humans in how to realize our natures as the particular kind of animals we are and possibly thus to achieve happy and flourishing lives. That to me seems very well suited for the human condition as understood to exist in an atheist universe.

Aristotelian ethics can form people, including those who believe they live in a godless cosmos, and motivate them to learn and to practice important and admirable moral virtues: prudence, courage, temperance, liberality, magnificence, magnanimity, proper ambition, pride in self, patience, good temper, truthfulness, wittiness, friendliness, modesty, and so on. These virtues may not propel people to the moral humanitarian heights of egalitarian sharing, universal benevolence, and the protected human rights of all people. But, by my lights, if most of humanity "only" managed to master Aristotelian virtues, that would be a huge moral achievement. And in the process, Aristotelian atheists could enjoy knowing that their arguments for being "good without God" were intellectually honest and rationally warranted.

Why then do atheists—at least those I engage in this book—ignore Aristotle? If he is the promising atheist ally I have described, why does he not show up on their radar screens? I do not know. I do, however, have a few hunches. These may or may not be correct, but perhaps they are worth mentioning.

Contemporary atheists are creatures of Enlightenment modernity (and some perhaps of postmodernism). So they feel much at home with the likes of Kant, Mill, and Bentham and sometimes with sanitized versions of Nietzsche. Aristotle is an ancient figure from the classical Mediterranean world. He also played a central role in the Thomistic theological synthesis of high medieval Christendom. His teleological natural philosophy was forcefully expunged from early modern science in the seventeenth century and has been disdained for centuries. For those reasons, Aristotle may seem to contemporary atheists alien and suspect. However, Aristotelian virtue ethics have enjoyed a resurgence of interest and influence in recent decades. Why hasn't that shown up in atheist arguments about ethics?

One reason may be that Aristotle does not buy them the very high moral standards they want to be able to promise and deliver on. What I view as an advantage of Aristotle for atheist ethics—namely, its substantial but not unrealistic moral aspirations—simply may not satisfy atheists. If so, then such atheists are making the nearly perfect the enemy of the attainable good. They are shooting for ethical heights they cannot ascend or defend, rather than accepting admirable but more realistic possibilities. That hardly comports with most atheists' self-image as unflinching realists, nor will it prove to be helpful to anyone over time.

I can think of another possible reason why Aristotle's ethics may not sit well with contemporary atheists. As Enlightenment moderns (and sometimes postmoderns), most atheists seem committed to helping emancipate individuals to live unconstrained lives of self-directed autonomy. That, of course, demands behaving ethically so that other individuals can also live free too. But it appears to me that individual autonomy through emancipation remains for most atheists the highest good, because freedom is believed to produce happiness. Without God to love and obey, individual human freedom becomes paramount; and whatever social conditions are necessary to maintain it (such as communities of morally good people) become an instrumental necessity. Each person should be able to determine her or his own individual telos.

Aristotle is not about emancipation and autonomy—at least not as Enlightenment moderns understand it. For Aristotle, the highest good is not freedom but happiness. And achieving happiness, he says, requires not emancipation from external influences but learning how to comport oneself well amid the naturally given forces and constraints that operate in our material, biological, and social realities. Aristotle says that true happiness comes when novices submit themselves to the authority of and follow the examples of those more accomplished in the virtues—to masters, who can teach through long and hard practice the dispositions, habits, and character necessary to realize proper human ends. I imagine that picture is not very appealing to modern atheists.

In Aristotelian ethics, the influences, structures, and tendencies of objective reality are not to be escaped through emancipation but are to be accepted as the inescapable context in which one can learn moral character through the lifelong practice of the virtues to achieve one's proper *telos* of happiness. Real happiness springs from virtuous living in naturally given contexts, not liberation from those contexts.[3] In the end, Aristotle would say, the virtuous are indeed emancipated, but emancipated from their base, stupid, ungoverned, animal propensities, not from external constraints per se. So if, as it seems to me, contemporary atheism is committed to a quite different humanistic, spiritual quest for individual emancipation, freedom, and self-determination, Aristotle would also not be appealing for this reason.[4]

This is all speculation. But whatever the reasons, I do think it strange that atheists today wishing to make the case for being "good without God" largely ignore Aristotelian virtue ethics. And sorting out the reasons why might help us better understand the deeper moral interests, commitments, and perhaps blind spots of contemporary atheists.

TO CLOSE

This book is clearly not the definitive word on atheism's prospects and limits. Nor is it intended as a work of academic guild philosophy. All of the issues addressed here we should view as matters of ongoing public conversations. Why? Because these issues have important practical social ramifications for our common life in the public sphere, and because they are intrinsically interesting and instructive. These are just the sorts of things about which citizens of healthy democracies ought to be learning and arguing well. Healthy democracies and societies require informed, critically thinking citizens and members. Demagoguery, cultural polarization, and political breakdown feed on simplistic views, narrow ideological thinking, and the inability to be openly self-critical. All parties involved in the theism-atheism debates, in shared moral reflection, and in the public consumption of the findings of science should be interested in and committed to careful reasoning, rigorous criticism, and the making of justified and defensible claims. To help advance those goods and to stimulate fruitful conversations, this book invites a broad audience—particularly college students and the reading public—to think about and participate in better-informed deliberations about atheism, morality, science, and human nature. If we can all learn to do that better, we will all be better off.

NOTES

Introduction

1. See, for example, David Voas and Mark Chaves, 2016, "Is the United States a Counterexample to the Secularization Thesis?," *American Journal of Sociology* 121(5): 1517–1556; Michael Hout and Claude Fischer, 2002, "Why More Americans Have No Religious Preference: Politics and Generations," *American Sociological Review* 67(2): 165–190.
2. More than a few nonfundamentalist religious leaders have noted and responded to this developing trend. See, for instance, Rod Dreher, 2017, *The Benedict Option: A Strategy for Christians in a Post-Christian Nation*. New York: Sentinel; Charles Chaput, 2017, *Strangers in a Strange Land: Living the Catholic Faith in a Post-Christian World*. New York: Holt; Anthony Esolen, 2017, *Out of the Ashes: Rebuilding American Culture*. Washington, DC: Regnery; Stanley Hauerwas, 2014, *Resident Aliens: Life in the Christian Colony*. Nashville: Abingdon Press.
3. To be clear, atheism is only one facet of the much larger and more complex phenomenon of secularization. Atheism ought to be understood as one aspect of secularization, but the latter cannot and should not be reduced to the former. This book focuses on atheist intellectual arguments; I have written elsewhere about secularization, in Christian Smith, 2017, *Religion: What It Is, How It Works, and Why It Matters*. Princeton: Princeton University Press.
4. One chapter does involve a critical review of some of the arguments of one of Sam Harris's books on science and morality.

5. Three of the four chapters have been published previously in different form in various other, relatively more obscure print outlets—which few of this book's readers will have had occasion to notice. The previous publication references are, where applicable, cited in the notes to each chapter.

6. At some point, however, the sophistication of professional guild philosophy can become counterproductive, per the discerning observation of University of Toronto professor of philosophy and classics John Rist: "the major issues in moral philosophy . . . are comparatively simple and cannot be fudged. Much of the sheer complication and difficulty of contemporary moral philosophy serves to blur this simplicity." Rist, 2002, *Real Ethics: Rethinking the Foundation of Morality*. Cambridge: Cambridge University Press, p. 8.

Chapter 1

1. The empirical question of how religious and secular groups compare morally, however, is far from settled. Simply to observe that atheists often are morally good does not itself answer the question of whether they tend as a population to be as good as or better than religious believers. For an example of empirical tests of these questions, see John H. Evans, 2016, *What Is a Human?* New York: Oxford University Press, pp. 49–70, 197–206.

2. Nonetheless, Paul Kurtz bases nearly his entire argument that atheists can be good without God on this empirical observation of goodness: that while "millions of people do not believe in God," still "they do believe very deeply in morality" and "have led exemplary lives of nobility and excellence, and . . . have contributed greatly to the common good." Kurtz, 2009, "The Kurtz/Craig Debate," in Robert Garcia and Nathan King (eds.), *Is Goodness without God Good Enough?* Lanham, MD: Rowman and Littlefield, pp. 25–29, 33–36, 42–44.

3. Philip Kitcher, 2014, *Life after Faith: The Case for Secular Humanism*. New Haven: Yale University Press; Kitcher, 2011, *The Ethical Project*. Cambridge, MA: Harvard University Press; Sam Harris, 2010, *The Moral Landscape: How Science Can Determine Human Values*. New York: Free Press; Greg Epstein, 2009, *Good without God: What a Billion Nonreligious People Do Believe*. New York: Harper; Lex Bayer and John Figdor, 2014, *Atheist Mind, Humanist Heart: Rewriting the Ten Commandments for the Twenty-First Century*: Lanham, MD: Rowman and Littlefield.

4. Frans de Waal, 2013, *The Bonobo and the Atheist*. New York: Norton; Phil Zuckerman, 2014, *Living the Secular Life*. New York: Penguin; Katherine Ozment, 2016, *Grace without God*. New York: Harper; Walter Sinnott-Armstrong, 2009, *Morality without God?* New York: Oxford University Press; Kai Nielsen, 1990. *Ethics without God*. Buffalo, NY: Prometheus; Ronald

Lindsay, 2014, *The Necessity of Secularism*. Durham, NC: Pitchstone. I also read and at times reference chapters in Garcia and King.

5. Here I align myself with the position philosophers call "reason externalism" (against "reason internalism"), which I think is the more rationally defensible and empirically realistic position. Colloquially said, reason externalism in ethics believes that motivations for moral action sometimes need to come from outside of the explanation for or judgment concerning why an action is right or good; reason internalism believes motivations are always internal to the moral judgment or explanation. Externalism is often associated with a Humean theory of action (beliefs + desires → actions), while internalism is often associated with a Kantian account (right beliefs → actions), among others. Russ Shafer-Landau provides what to me are convincing arguments for reason externalism in his 2003 book *Moral Realism* (New York: Oxford University Press, pp. 119–161), concluding that "whether attention to any given fact generates motivation depends on what else is in an agent's motivational profile. . . . A deeply immoral person, even after being confronted with the moral truth, may nevertheless remain indifferent to it. . . . Amoralism is a genuine possibility: one may sincerely endorse the rightness of an action without thereby being motivated to perform it. . . . It is at least conceptually possible for a sincere normative judgment to entirely lack motivational power. . . . We are misled if we move from the obvious fact that moral judgments are usually motivating, to the stronger claim that they cannot fail to be" (pp. 120, 121, 145, 161).

6. Why do I believe Kantians (and, more broadly, reason internalists) are wrong here? Answering that question adequately is beyond the scope of this book, so here I only offer a few basic thoughts. To begin, let us remind ourselves that Kant was no secularist, despite his critiques of traditional arguments for the existence of God. Kant viewed as essential for the success of his rationalist ethics the postulates of the existence of (1) an omnipotent, omniscient, and just divinity, and (2) an afterlife and some kind of immortality of the human soul. (See, for example, Chris Surprenant, 2008, "Kant's Postulate of the Immortality of the Soul," *International Philosophical Quarterly* 48(1): 85–98; Christopher Insole, 2016, *The Intolerable God: Kant's Theological Journey*. Grand Rapids, MI: Eerdmans). This means that atheist Kantian ethicists today who think they can simply delete Kant's explicit reliance on a divinity and an afterlife, and still make work his principle that the justifying motivation to act rightly is simply contained in a rational warranting explanation for the right, are claiming an accomplishment Kant himself thought impossible. By my lights, the divinity and afterlife that Kant believed necessary for his ethics to work function practically as the ultimate backstop motivating factor situating the moral agent, meaning that my position here may actually not be too far off from his own.

We must also understand in the developing history of ideas that Kant's insistence that the motivation to act morally is provided simply by a rational warranting explanation for the right was specifically set in opposition to the contrary position against which he was arguing, namely David Hume's empiricist ethics. Important about that for present purposes is that Hume's characteristically consistent empiricist case, centered on human passions, drove the dissenting Kant to develop his characteristically consistent rationalist case, centered on the a priori categorical imperative. Kant was determined that his universalist ethics would involve no contingent, a posteriori feature, so what counts as a good reason for moral actions could not require an additional element of a justification for motivation. Paul Guyer, 2008, *Knowledge, Reason, and Taste: Kant's Responses to Hume*, Princeton: Princeton University Press. Warranted explanations of the right alone must propel moral actions, for example: "everyone must grant that a law, if it is to hold morally, that is, as a ground of an obligation, it must carry with it absolute necessity. . . . Therefore, the ground of obligation . . . must not be sought in the nature of the human being or in the circumstances of the world in which he is placed, but a priori simply in concepts of pure reason." *Groundwork of the Metaphysics of Morals*, in *Practical Philosophy*, 1996 (1785), trans. and ed. Mary Gregor. Cambridge: Cambridge University Press, 4:389. That was a move of *logical* necessity for Kant, given his case against Hume, but, I suggest, it was not well matched to the *actual* subjects of moral actions, namely, real, empirical human beings. Knowing how complex actual processes of human cognition and motivation are, we have very good prima facie reason to be suspicious of an ethical system that is as one-sided as either Hume's or Kant's, however internally consistently they were argued.

I count myself among philosophers like Barbara Herman, Paul Guyer, and Allen Wood who question the success of Kant's program of reliance on the motivational capacity of rational warrant alone, apart from the need for an associated element of some value justifying moral motivations. Herman, 1993, *The Practice of Moral Judgment*. Cambridge, MA: Harvard University Press; Guyer and Wood, 1998, introduction to Immanuel Kant, *Critique of Pure Reason*, trans. Paul Guyer and Allen Wood. Cambridge: Cambridge University Press; Wood, 1999, *Kant's Ethical Thought*. New York: Cambridge University Press. Such arguments, if I read them correctly, suggest that Kant's exclusive insistence on the right over the good fails to acknowledge a values teleology present in, or at least implied by, the structure of his argument. If nothing else, the motivating desire of the erstwhile moral skeptic not to violate her own rational agency or autonomy or humanity itself must serve as value-leverage external to the rational warrant of the right, needed to overcome the possible resistance and be motivated actually to choose and act on the right in the duty of good will.

At bottom, I am here considering two fundamentally different philosophical views of the relationship of human reason and will. For Kant, the rational will is the good will, so to be properly rational is necessarily to be good. Painting with a broad brush, we may call this the Platonic tradition, in which immoral behavior results from ignorance, error, or irrationality. The alternative historical tradition, which we might call Augustinian, recognizes a crucial disjunct between reason and will, and locates much immoral behavior not in a flaw in reason but primarily in the misdirection of the will. In the latter tradition, reason can conclude whatever it wishes, but the will has at least a semiautonomy of its own to motivate contrary behaviors to which it might be attracted. This outlook does not need to swing all the way over to Hume's view of reason as always the "slave of the passions." (This view itself is a secularized version of Martin Luther's view, expressed in his 1525 work *On the Bondage of the Will*, which differed significantly from the *pietistic* Lutheranism in which Kant was raised, which instead emphasized the self-control of one's will, duty to the right, self-purification from besetting sinful influences, methodical sanctification, and so on and which figured so influentially as background sensibilities in his later ethics.) And purely on the grounds of realistic empirical observation, not theological inclination, I think something like the Augustinian account of the relation of reason and will is manifestly more apt than the Platonic account. And so I think Kant is operating on faulty premises on this critical issue.

This helps to explain why, empirically, the behavior of few if any people is governed primarily by rationalist philosophical proofs. Whether or not reason is capable of independently determining the will for some, it does not for most of humanity. Nor would it, I think, even if everyone read and understood Kantian ethics. This position is also validated by mounds of cognitive science scholarship in recent decades on the subsidiary role of reflective reasoning in the empirical processes of human moral decision-making. (The literature on this is immense, but for starters see Jonathan Haidt, 2006, *The Happiness Hypothesis*. New York: Basic Books; Haidt, 2012, *The Righteous Mind*. New York: Pantheon.) So the reasonable skeptics and the "sensible knaves" I discuss below may actually understand the rational argument why some action ought to be judged to be wrong, but still lack the motivational component of a justifying reason to care about it enough to mobilize their wills actually to do what is right. The Kantian will object: "but that is a violation of basic rationality, which is what sets us apart from brute animals and is the condition of the possibility of any intelligible social life!" Much of humanity, if it even cares to answer, will reply: "okay, whatever." In short, Kantianism is an elegant ethical system, but—especially when the divinity and afterlife, which Kant thought were essential for its success, are removed—it is ill-suited for the actual creatures whom philosophical ethics exist to form: real human beings. In order to "be good," real, empirical people not only philosophical ideal types—require both warranting explanations and motivational justifications.

Of course, Kant himself was not oblivious to this. Kant was unduly sanguine about the extent of moral agreement among sound, normal, adult human persons in different cultures (and not simply from his perspective in eighteenth-century

Königsberg, Germany). Nevertheless, he actually expressed doubts in his writings as to whether any human actions have ever been motivated by the sheer force of duty (for example, *Groundwork*, 4:406–407). And, perhaps sensing a vulnerability in his earlier works for such reasons, Kant's account of the role of emotions in fostering morality expressed in his latter writings complicates the simple view emphasizing the sufficiency of good will alone (see Guyer 2008; 2010, "Moral Feelings in the *Metaphysics of Morals*," in Lara Denis (ed.), *Kant's Metaphysics of Morals: A Critical Guide*, Cambridge: Cambridge University Press, pp. 130–151). Thus, the "Kantian" view may not be as clear-cut as some latter-day Kantians might imagine or hope.

7. For present purposes, I follow these atheist moralists in treating "moral" and "good" as interchangeable, even though a more precise analysis would need to distinguish them.

8. Bayer and Figdor 110; Kitcher 2014: 64; Epstein 93.

9. Harris 55, 65, 79–80, 106, 110; Kitcher 2014: 58; 2001: 17, 82, 255, 409; Epstein 21, 118; Beyer and Figdor 92, 93, 97; also see Zuckerman 13; de Waal 49, 156; Lindsay 77–78.

10. Harris 55, 106, 110, 191; Kitcher 2014: 53, 87–88; Epstein xviii, 25, 118; Beyer and Figdor 94, 110, 139; also see Zuckerman 13, 15, 20, 36.

11. Bayer and Figdor 97; Epstein xviii. They do not distinguish between doing the good to others we want done to ourselves (the *golden* rule of Jesus) and not doing the bad to others we do not want done to ourselves (the so-called *silver* rule of Rabbi Hillel and Confucius), which is a big ethical difference, but for present purposes let us set that aside. See Doug Porpora, 2001, *Landscapes of the Soul*. New York: Oxford University Press. Zuckerman writes: "What is good? . . . Simple: the Golden Rule. . . . Treating others as you would like to be treated. . . . Not harming others and helping those in need . . . which flow easily and directly from . . . the simple logic of empathetic reciprocity" (13). Frans de Waal is the only one of these authors who explicitly rejects the Golden Rule as an inadequate moral guide, on the grounds that it has the fatal flaw of assuming that what others want is the same as what we want ("that all people are alike") and that, due to its "very limited reach," it "doesn't help resolve most [moral] dilemmas" (181–182).

12. Quotes in this paragraph come from Kitcher 2014, 158; 2011, 304, 367, 374–375, 376, 396.

13. Quotes from this paragraph come from Epstein 223, 224, 225, 146–150.

14. Harris 28, 36, 43, 50, 52.

15. Beyer and Figdor 106. Others agree. The atheist philosopher Kai Nielsen, for instance, claims that "morality requires that we attempt to distribute happiness as evenly as possible. We must be fair. . . . Requirements of justice make it necessary that each person be given equal consideration" (Nielsen 122).

16. Also see Stephen Law, 2013, "Humanism," in Stephen Bullivant and Michael Ruse (eds.), *The Oxford Handbook of Atheism*. New York: Oxford University Press, pp. 263–277.

17. Nielsen says: "our individual welfare is dependent upon having a device [morality] that equitably resolves social and individual conflict" (126). Lindsay writes that morality "creates stability, provides security, ameliorates harmful conditions, fosters trust, and facilitates cooperation in achieving shared and complementary goals. . . . Morality enables us to live together and . . . improve the conditions under which we live" (77–78).

18. Nielsen actually conflates deontological and functionalist ethics: "the Kantian principle of respect for persons is actually bound up in the very idea . . . that our individual welfare is dependent on having a device that equitably resolves social and individual conflicts" (126).

19. Harris 65, 110, 191.

20. Bayer and Figdor 107. The following quotes in this paragraph come from 89, 92, 96, 95, 97, 110, 139.

21. Epstein 35; the following quote p. 34. Margaret Knight says: "why should I consider others? . . . I think the only possible answer to this question is the Humanist one—because we are naturally social beings; we live in communities; and life in any community, from the family outwards, is much happier, and fuller, and richer if its members are friendly and cooperative than if they are hostile and resentful" (quoted in Law, 2013, 271).

22. Epstein 103. Unclear throughout Epstein's writings, however, remains the question of whether we should by social contract treat people *as if* they have dignity because we prefer that—as is suggested by much of his language about dignity needing to be "promoted," "struggled for," "cultivated," "a goal to strive for," and, indeed, about humans as having "the *potential* for dignity" (37, 89, 90, 91)—or instead take the realist position that people should be treated well because they are objectively endowed with a *real* dignity that as a moral fact must be honored, whether or not anyone does so.

23. For the most part, the arguments are straightforwardly honest in acknowledging that if God and/or some moral natural law do not exist, then what we think of as morality really is a human construction, with no external, objective reference. (I do not think they take the implications of that premise seriously enough, but at least they are unflinchingly clear about the premise.) I also largely agree with these writers' arguments against the modern rejection of the so-called naturalistic fallacy, inherited from (a misreading of) Hume, which insists that facts and values must be divorced. To make their cases, these atheist moralists must show that morality derives from the facts of human life, and so they must undercut modernity's rejection of the naturalistic fallacy. Values, they must show, are informed by facts. My own neo-Aristotelian critical realist personalism agrees with them on this point. (See Smith, 2010,

What Is a Person?: Rethinking Humanity, Social Life, and the Moral Good from the Person Up. Chicago: University of Chicago Press; Smith, 2015, *To Flourish or Destruct: A Personalist Theory of Human Goods, Motivations, Failure, and Evil.* Chicago: University of Chicago Press.) I think that some of these atheist moralists do a better job than most moral philosophers today in taking seriously what we can learn from relevant social scientific, cognitive, and neurological research relevant to moral behavior. They go overboard at times, but in general I appreciate that some of them try to take relevant science seriously.

24. Kitcher 2011, 316, 317, italics added for emphasis; the following quote is 314–315, italics in original.

25. Kitcher 2014, 51, italics added for emphasis. Likewise, Nielsen insists on "the need to do what we can to diminish the awful sum of human misery in the world." He adds: "morality requires that we attempt to distribute happiness as evenly as possible. We must be fair: each person is to count for one and none is to count for more than one." Nielsen. 1990, *Ethics without God.* Buffalo, NY: Prometheus Books, p. 117.

26. Nielsen 34, 148, 223, 224, 225, italics added.

27. Harris 52, 7.

28. Bayer and Figdor 106, 71, 92; the next quotes come from 109, 139, 140, and 114–115.

29. Bayer and Figdor center *autonomous individual preference and choice* as their highest moral value, including in determining whether to adhere to any moral norms, even against murder. This puts them in a bind when it comes to dealing with those who choose not to be "good" by their standards (e.g., Bayer and Figdor 89, 97, 98, 106). All they can do is try to persuade others that the choice to be "bad" will lead to their own unhappiness. If that fails, they have no other noncoercive recourse, and coercion violates individual choice.

30. Kitcher 2011, 304, 305.

31. Similarly, the moral philosopher Ronald Lindsay explains for those who "want an explanation of the reason for acknowledging moral obligations": "it's largely a matter of logical consistency. *If* we accept the institution of morality, then we are tacitly agreeing to be bound by its norms. We cannot logically maintain that moral norms apply to everyone except us." More Lindsay: "in saying an action is morally wrong, we are committed to making the same judgment regardless of whether it is I or someone else doing the action" (Lindsay 110). The dubious rationalist presupposition here, again, is that human behavior is straightforwardly driven by logic and the desire for rational consistency, which neither convinces me nor, I am confident, reasonable skeptics.

32. If Kitcher had wanted to succeed, he would have needed to supply more explicit premises to connect his argument to its conclusion, such as (1) the increased connectedness of a globalized world means that the well-being of

every other society and person on the planet actually does affect every other person's well-being, or (2) all humans are highly morally responsible for not only their own lives and those of their children but also for many generations of humans into the future. But I do not think either of these would be or need to be plausible premises to the reasonable skeptic.

33. Bayer and Figdor promise to address the challenge of universal inclusion in chapter 11 of their book, but they end up only discussing how to weigh trade-offs of goods between different people, which is a different matter.

34. Charles Taylor asks: "is the naturalist affirmation conditional on a vision of human nature in the fullness of its health and strength? Does it move us to extend help to the irremediably broken, such as the mentally handicapped, those dying without dignity, fetuses with genetic defects?" Taylor, 1989, *Sources of the Self*. Cambridge, MA: Harvard University Press, p. 516.

35. "High standards need strong sources. This is because there is something morally corrupting, even dangerous, in sustaining the demand simply on the feeling of undischarged obligation, on guilt, or its obverse, self-satisfaction" (Taylor 516).

36. See note 6.

37. Hume: "according to the imperfect ways in which human affairs are conducted, a sensible knave, in particular incidents, may think, that an act of iniquity or infidelity will make a considerable addition to his fortune, without causing any considerable breach in the social union or confederacy. That honesty is the best policy may be a good general rule; but is liable to many exceptions: And he, it may, perhaps, be thought, conducts himself with most wisdom, who observes the general rule, and takes advantage of all the exceptions." That is the difficulty. Hume admits: "I must confess that, if a man think[s] that this reasoning much requires an answer, it will be a little difficult to find any which will to him appear satisfactory and convincing." Hume, 1983, *An Enquiry Concerning Principles of Morals*. Indianapolis: Hackett, p. 81.

38. To formalize this, the "sensible knave" scenario requires three joint conditions and is enhanced by a fourth: (1) knave almost always upholds moral norms and thus develops a reputation for being good, honest, and reliable; (2) knave privately monitors situations to recognize exceptional opportunities in which (a) violating moral norms would (b) provide significant self-serving advantages (c) at very low risks of being caught; and (3) knave is mentally and emotionally prepared to capitalize upon such situations without hesitation (in contrast to what would be expected based on knave's public reputation) in order to maximize the chances of success. Knave is psychologically aided in this by (4) understanding the conditions and consequences of atheism (e.g., that moral norms are only human inventions, that one only need fear being caught, not the judgments of God or the inexorable consequences of karma or some other natural law or superhuman force).

39. Some social scientists have tried to solve the free rider problem by appealing to "selective incentives," but these can only contribute partially to other reasons not to free ride and never alone make that decision justified.

40. David Brink in *The Cambridge Companion to Atheism*: "The question really asks about the *rational authority of morality*. That question arises for most of us because of a perceived tension between the other-regarding demands of morality and a broadly prudential conception of practical reason, according to which what one has reason to do is to promote one's own aims or interests. For meeting the demands of nonaggression, cooperation, fidelity, fair play, and charity often appears to constrain one's pursuit of one's own aims or interests .... As long as we understand the prudential justification of morality in terms of instrumental advantage, the secular coincidence between other-regarding morality and enlightened self-interest must remain imperfect. Sometimes non-compliance would go undetected; and even where noncompliance is detected, the benefits ... sometimes outweigh the costs.... Compliance involves costs as well as benefits. It must remain a second-best option, behind undetected non-compliance, in which one enjoys the benefits of others' compliance without the costs of one's own." Brink, 2007, "The Autonomy of Ethics," in Michael Martin (ed.), *The Cambridge Companion to Atheism*. Cambridge: Cambridge University Press, pp. 160–161, italics in original. Also see Candace Vogler, 2009, *Reasonably Vicious*. Cambridge, MA: Harvard University Press.

41. Hume's reply, for example: "in all ingenuous natures, the antipathy to treachery and roguery is too strong to be counterbalanced by any views of profit or pecuniary advantage. Inward peace of mind, consciousness of integrity, a satisfactory review of our own conduct; these are circumstances very requisite to happiness, and will be cherished and cultivated by every honest man, who feels the importance of them. Such a one has, besides, the frequent satisfaction of seeing knaves, with all their pretending cunning and ability, betrayed by their own maxims" (Hume 82). For "honest men" to act like sensible knaves, they will "have sacrificed the invaluable enjoyments of a character ... for the acquisition of worthless toys and gewgaws ... above all the peaceful reflection of one's own conduct" (82). MacIntyre rightly inquires: "Why should we obey rules on occasions when it is not to our interest to do so? Hume ... tries to conclude that it is to our long-term advantage to be just, when all that his premises warrant is the ... conclusion that it is often to our long-term advantage that people *generally* should be just. And [Hume] has to evoke ... what he calls 'the communicated passion of sympathy': [that] we find it agreeable that some quality is agreeable to others because we are so constructed that we naturally sympathize with those others. The ... [more honest] answer would have been: 'Sometimes we do, sometimes we do not; and when we do not, why should we?'" MacIntyre, 1984, *After Virtue*. Notre Dame, IN: University of Notre Dame Press, pp. 229–230, italics added.

42. All quotes following come from Kitcher 2011, 275–276; 2014, 56.

43. Sinnott-Armstrong similarly claims that "it is normally to be in our interest to be moral. Immorality rarely pays. . . . Even when [cheaters] get away with it, they usually won't be happier, or much happier, than if they had made more modest gains honestly. They will often be hounded by guilt or fear of rivals or of punishment" (Sinnott-Armstrong 114).

44. Bayer and Figdor 109, 110, italics added for emphasis.

45. Kitcher 2011, 87.

46. Here we see slippage between the need for people to be truly, consistently honest, despite the costs, and merely developing a reputation for trustworthiness. De Waal for example speaks about "*reputations* of honesty and trustworthiness" (234); and Bayer and Figdor talk of people who have the "desire *to be seen as* an honest person" (97).

47. Kitcher 2011, 276.

48. Harris 40, 68.

49. "There is no one way we 'ought to behave.' We choose to behave in the way we think optimizes our life-happiness" (Bayer and Figdor 89).

50. MacIntyre demonstrates a similar dynamic in Hume, whereby his internal incoherence is driven by "two incompatible attitudes" he held: "on the one hand, Hume insists that there is nothing to judgments of virtue and vice except the expression of feelings of approval and disapproval. Thus there can be no criteria external to those feelings by appeal to which we may pass judgement on them. . . . Yet at the same time he wishes to condemn, sometimes in the harshest of terms, those who hold certain alternative views of the virtues" (230–231). It doesn't add up.

51. Bayer and Figdor 96, italics added for emphasis.

52. Harris 56, italics added for emphasis. Harris also says: "we feel guilt/shame over our own moral failings" (92). Yes, often we do, but *not always*, and especially not when we are convinced that we have done nothing objectively wrong.

53. Bayer and Figdor 93. Similarly: "cooperative action can be a way for someone to maximize his or her own self-interest." The next quote comes from 97, italics added for emphasis.

54. Again, Bayer and Figdor claim that "we benefit from living in and supporting an ethical society" (110). True, generally. But to this the sensible knave can also say to himself, not erroneously, "yes, and *I* benefit *even more* when I support it most of the time and then take careful advantage of it in propitious situations."

55. Harris 42, italics in original. Harris recurrently argues by referencing extremes in statements such as this: "it is good to avoid behaving in such a way as to produce the *worst possible misery for everyone*" (39, italics added).

56. Epstein 91. Similarly, Lindsay frames what are allegedly the only two alternatives available in the extreme, as either completely "accepting the institutions of morality . . . and accepting the obligations that come with this

institution" (which requires consistent obedience) or "rejecting the institution of morality *entirely*" (meaning "to cut oneself off from human society")—thus pretending that the sensible knave option does not exist (Lindsay 110, 111, italics added for emphasis).

57. Sinnott-Armstrong illustrates more sidestepping, by answering the question of why people should be moral even when it fails to serve their personal interests simply by disconnecting "reasons" from "motivations" (instead of, in good Kantian fashion, directly embedding moral motivations in the warranting reasons). The "obvious" reason to act morally, he says, is this: "the fact that an act causes harm to others is reason not to do that act, and the fact that an act prevents harm to others is a reason to do that act. There is, then, always a reason to be moral on this secular account." But why, the reasonable skeptic might ask, should I *care* about preventing harm to others? Well, *that*, replies Sinnott-Armstrong, is a *totally different question*, one concerning motivations. "Some rapists may not care about harming others," he notes. "However, all that shows is that they lack the motivation to be moral. Motives are crucially different from reasons." The rapist actually still has a good reason not to commit rape, he says, in order not to harm the victim, which "it would not be irrational or crazy" to act upon. Thus, "there is a *reason* for them to be moral, even if it takes *something else*—such as good character or training—to *motivate* them to be moral. . . . For people who really do not care about others, the solution is found in retraining and restraining rather than in theory" (pp. 117, 118). Essentially, Sinnott-Armstrong is saying that secularism can provide good, rational reasons to be ethical, but that whether or not it can motivate people actually to act ethically is a different question that someone else is responsible to answer. And that seems to me, in the real world, to be an indirect admission of failure.

58. Kitcher 2014, 47, 48.

59. Kitcher 2014, 142, 143, 153–154. Note how Kitcher's introduction of the words "inevitable" and "ineradicability" exemplifies the rhetorical dodge of going to extremes described above. His shift from "remembering the extent of cruelty in human history" (142) to talk of "*hypothetical* tendencies" is another sleight of hand. And given that humans have perfected the technology for total self-annihilation and continue in global political struggles to flirt with that possibility, the language of "premature" here seems ill-chosen.

60. Epstein 125.

61. Bayer and Figdor 114. Is the dehumanizing of other really only "sad"?

62. Bayer and Figdor 117–118. Bayer and Figdor place massive faith in the power of talking things out: "even without an absolute moral truth, we can still have meaningful conversations about right and wrong actions. It's true that claims about right and wrong can't be stated as certainties, but they can be stated as strong (and even enforceable) preferences. As a result, we can still debate

ethical values by relating the preferences of the individual to the moral consensus preferences of society—that is, balancing what you want against what's best for society"; and "the mere fact that our opinions and your opinions are both subjective doesn't mean we can't sensibly debate between the two.... You might just convince us that your reasons are a better fit even for our own self-interest" (92, 105).

63. Epstein 139; here Epstein is endorsing an argument of Alan Dershowitz.
64. Ozment 70, 115.
65. Epstein 56.
66. A different line of interrogation of these writings would examine the extent to which the content of their moral systems is parasitically dependent upon the Western Jewish and Christian heritage of morality that they inherit from two millennia of Christendom and more of Judaism. Atheists may reply: "it may well be the case that, as a historical fact, our moral concern for persons came from our religious conceptions, but it is a well-known principle of logic that the validity of a belief is independent of its origin. What the religious moralist must do is show that only on religious grounds could such a principle of respect for persons be justifiably asserted. But he has not shown this is so" (Nielsen 123). This inquiry is worth exploring but is not my primary concern here.
67. Bayer and Figdor 107.
68. The difficulties on which I have focused above are by no means the only problems besetting these atheist moralists. All of these writers also indulge in expressions of vulgar empiricist scientism, basing allegedly knock-down arguments against religion on naïve and outdated epistemological assumptions. Moreover, they all display (what should be) embarrassing ignorance of the variety and nuances of religious accounts for human morality, substituting caricatures of divine-command theory that they assume are easily defeated by the "Euthyphro dilemma." They display an incredible neglect of Aristotle, whose virtue ethics could present them with both great help and significant challenges. Some of these writers tend to confuse the question of whether atheists have reasons to be morally good with the distinct question of whether atheists can lead *meaningful* or *purpose-filled* lives—thus failing to recognize that one could well lead a meaningful life that is anything but morally good (e.g., I have no doubt that the lives of many Nazi fascists were highly meaningful). Many of these atheist moralists exhibit a captivity to the incoherent moral emotivism criticized by Alasdair MacIntyre: they declare gratuitous negative moral judgments (of things they do not like as "crass," "sad," "misled," "unfortunate," "unhealthy," "elitist," "cruel," "silly," and "misguided") that are unjustifiable by their own moral systems. Some of these atheist moralists shift inconsistently between the view that our evolutionary inheritance is a nearly determinative control shaping our lives on the one hand and the view that we

humans are free to transcend as we please the dictates of our evolutionarily inherited traits on the other as our purposes dictate (e.g., Harris says of our evolved functional "penchant for out-group hostility" that "such evolutionary constraints no longer hold. . . . We are now poised to consciously engineer our further evolution"; 102). Most of these writers treat all moral questions as a matter of how people treat one another in interpersonal relationships (e.g., Frans de Waal says: "morality is a system of rules concerning the two H's of Helping or at least not Hurting fellow human beings. It addresses the well-being of others and puts the community before the individual"; 156), which reductively truncates the way most cultures and philosophers have conceived of ethics and morality. Those who emphasize human happiness treat, in good utilitarian fashion, everyone's search for happiness as similar; they fail to recognize how perceptions of the content of and best strategies for achieving happiness and well-being depend very heavily on people's locations in social structures and institutions, a fact that greatly complicates the kind of aggregations of happiness that utilitarians seek. And these atheist moralists are also oddly obsessed with hell, when few contemporary religious people, including American evangelicals, talk much about the subject.

69. Taylor 517.
70. Z. Kunda, 1990, "The Case for Motivated Reasoning," *Psychological Bulletin* 108(3): 480–498; L. Nir, 2011, "Motivated Reasoning and Public Opinion Perception," *Public Opinion Quarterly* 75(3): 504.
71. Similarly, MacIntyre explains inconsistencies in Hume's moral account, which lacks any criteria of judgment beyond "the passions of men of good sense," thusly: his "appeal to a universal verdict by mankind turns out to be the mask worn by an appeal to those who physiologically and socially share Hume's attitudes and *Weltanschauung*. . . . What Hume identifies as the standpoint of universal human nature turns out in fact to be that of the prejudices of the Hanoverian ruling elite." His account is thus "an attempt to claim universal rational authority for what is in fact the local morality of parts of eighteenth-century Northern Europe" (231–232). This is related to what Charles Taylor calls a "subtraction story" of secularization, namely, the view that we can retain a liberal humanism inherited in part from millennia of religious influences even after we subtract God from the picture. Taylor, 2007, *A Secular Age*. Cambridge, MA: Harvard University Press.
72. Charles Taylor has said: "only if there is such a thing as agape, or one of the secular claimants to its succession, is Nietzsche wrong" (Taylor 1989, 516). I suppose at issue there is what could count as a "secular claimant" to succeed God's agape love. Also see Philip Yancey, 1998, "Nietzsche Was Right," *Books and Culture*, January/February, 14–17; David Bentley Hart, 2003, "Christ and Nothing," *First Things*, October, https://www.firstthings.com/article/2003/10/christ-and-nothing.

73. I have made tentative efforts to elaborate this idea in two books: *What Is a Person?* and *To Flourish or Destruct*. But see John Hare, 2009, "Is Moral Goodness without Belief in God Rationally Stable?," in Garcia and King 85–99.

Chapter 2

1. A shorter version of this chapter was previously published as "Does Naturalism Warrant a Moral Belief in Universal Benevolence and Human Rights?," in Jeffrey Schloss and Michael Murray (eds.), 2009, *The Believing Primate: Scientific, Philosophical and Theological Perspectives on the Evolution of Religion*. New York: Oxford University Press, pp. 292–316.
2. Michael Ruse, 2013, "Naturalism and the Scientific Method," in Stephen Bullivant and Michael Ruse (eds.), *The Oxford Handbook of Atheism*. New York: Oxford University Press, pp. 383–397.
3. Francis Collins, the former director of the Human Genome Project and director of the National Institute of Health, provides an example of one exception with his 2007 book *The Language of God: A Scientist Presents Evidence for Belief*. New York: Free Press.
4. Evan Fales, 2007, "Naturalism and Physicalism," in Michael Martin (ed.), *The Cambridge Companion to Atheism*. Cambridge: Cambridge University Press, pp. 118–134. Important to note is that the particular conceptions of "nature," "supernatural," and "transcendent" embedded in this position of naturalism are grounded in particular, Western, especially Abrahamic conceptions of God and religion in which God is the transcendent creator of and ruler over nature, which is itself not-God. Some other religions and quasi-religious philosophies understand spirits existing *as part of* nature per se or view the natural order of reality as involving some larger cosmic force (e.g., karma) that does not transcend but helps to constitute nature. Thus, these standard categories used by both theists and atheists in the West are not universally applicable but are historically and culturally located and are ultimately defined theologically.
5. In this, I follow in the path of philosophers like Nicholas Wolterstorff and Michael Perry, among others, who have argued that no stable nonreligious justification exists for a commitment to universal human rights. Wolterstorff, 2010, *Justice: Rights and Wrongs*. Princeton: Princeton University Press; Perry, 2000, *Human Rights: Four Inquiries*. New York: Oxford University Press; Perry, 2008, *Toward a Theory of Human Rights: Religion, Law, Courts*. Cambridge: Cambridge University Press.
6. Rodney Stark, 1997, *The Rise of Christianity*. HarperSanFrancisco; David Bentley Hart, 2010, *Atheist Delusions: The Christian Revolution and Its Fashionable Enemies*. New Haven: Yale University Press.

7. Elizabeth Kolbert, 2015, *The Sixth Extinction*. New York: Picador; Richard Posner, 2004, *Catastrophe: Risk and Response*. New York: Oxford University Press; Ted Koppel, 2015, *Lights Out*. New York: Crown; also see Joseph Tainter, 1988, *The Collapse of Complex Societies*. Cambridge: Cambridge University Press; Vaclav Smil, 2012, *Global Catastrophes and Trends: The Next 50 Years*. Cambridge, MA: MIT Press; Naomi Oreskes and Erik Conway, 2014, *The Collapse of Western Civilization: A View from the Future*. New York: Columbia University Press.

8. Charles Taylor, 1989, *Sources of the Self*. Cambridge, MA: Harvard University Press.

9. Christian Smith, 2003, *Moral, Believing Animals*. New York: Oxford University Press.

10. James Rachels: "we are not entitled—not on evolutionary grounds, at any rate—to regard our own adaptive behavior as 'better' or 'higher' than that of a cockroach, who, after all, is adapted equally well to life in its own environmental niche"; 1990, *Created from Animals: The Moral Implications of Darwinism*. New York: Oxford University Press, p. 70.

11. By this I mean not simply having an emotional reaction but practicing emotivism in its more precise meaning as discussed by Alasdair MacIntyre, 1981, *After Virtue: A Study in Moral Theory*. Notre Dame, IN: University of Notre Dame Press.

12. Smith, 2010 [1759], *The Theory of Moral Sentiments*. New York: Penguin Classics.

13. Emile Durkheim, 2014 [1893], *The Division of Labor in Society*. New York: Free Press.

14. For example, Singer, 1993, *Practical Ethics*. Cambridge: Cambridge University Press; Helga Kuhse and Peter Singer, 1986, *Should the Baby Live?* Studies in Bioethics. New York: Oxford University Press.

15. See, for example, Chris Surprenant, 2008, "Kant's Postulate of the Immortality of the Soul," *International Philosophical Quarterly* 48(1): 85–98; Christopher Insole, 2016, *The Intolerable God: Kant's Theological Journey*. Grand Rapids, MI: Eerdmans; "in effect, what Kant (and some of his successors) have done . . . is to retain the overriding claims of 'strict morality' and obedience to duty, originally backed by what was taken for God's will, and over against other (say, more Aristotelian) aspects of the 'good life,' within increasingly secularized moral systems. . . . Kant managed to retain the Christian claim that the good man is capable of self-unification (of which God is still the ultimate guarantor), but only by the agency of the purified moral will. . . . Kantianism fails without the hidden Christianity, and [that failure] points to the impossibility of an ethical theory which is both substantive and non-metaphysical." John Rist, 2002, *Real Ethics: Rethinking the Foundation of Morality*. Cambridge: Cambridge University Press, pp. 167, 176.

16. MacIntyre, 1981.

17. As John Rist observes: "how can I do my duty if I obtain no personal satis-faction *at all* from doing my duty? . . . Kant . . . must fall victim to Hume: if a dutiful man obtains no personal satisfaction from being dutiful, acting solely because it is his duty, he lacks motivation and *cannot* act at all. Kant condemns him to giving commands to himself which he has no intelligible motive and therefore no ability to obey." Rist 166, italics in original.

18. Russ Schafer-Landau, 2005, *Moral Realism: A Defence.* Cambridge, MA: Clarendon Press.

19. Schafer-Landau 2, 8.

20. Schafer-Landau 48.

21. Schafer-Landau 247. "Self-evident" does not mean that everyone must or will believe the moral principle, simply that it is justified for those who do (see pp. 256–265).

22. Schafer-Landau 248.

23. Schafer-Landau 55, italics in the original. By "naturalism," he means "a met-aphysical thesis about the nature of properties, [which] claims that all real properties are those that would figure ineliminably in perfected versions of the natural and social sciences" (59).

24. Schafer-Landau 63.

25. As Charles Lamore has also shown in his 1996 antinaturalist book *The Morals of Modernity.* Cambridge: Cambridge University Press.

26. Schafer-Landau 63, 66.

27. Schafer-Landau 66.

28. Schafer-Landau 79.

29. Schafer-Landau 76. "The properties that physicists find ineliminably useful are but a small set of those that we believe to be real" (76).

30. Schafer-Landau 76.

31. Schafer Landau 63, 66.

32. He seems, rightly, too intellectually cautious to venture such an ambitious claim. About his argument for even his limited list of self-evident moral facts, he admits: "I wish I could say I was fully confident of its merits," acknowledging that "knock-down, watertight philosophical arguments are always in very short supply." Schafer-Landau 8–9.

33. Erik Wielenberg has attempted to advance and defend a robust nonthe-istic, nonnaturalistic moral realism that explicitly attempts to vindicate (nonuniversal) human rights in his 2014 book *Robust Ethics: The Metaphysics and Epistemology of Godless Normative Realism.* New York: Oxford University Press. Like Shafer-Landau, Wielenberg does not believe ethics can be under-stood in naturalistic terms, so his is a *non*naturalistic account, agreeing with William FitzPatrick that strictly naturalistic accounts of morality "secure the 'reality' of ethical facts and properties only by turning them into something

else and deflating them in the process" (p. 15). The only part of naturalism Wielenberg is prepared to endorse is that he does not "reject the causal closure of the physical or deny that the physical sciences are entirely successful in their own domains" (pp. 15–16), a more circumscribed version than that under consideration in this chapter. Moreover, in his more typically cautious modes of argument, Wielenberg only seeks (like Shafer-Landau) to defend very modest moral facts—such as that it is morally wrong to torture other people merely for one's own pleasure—not the very ambitious moral claims of universal benevolence and human rights. Even so, as his argument unfolds, Wielenberg eventually does venture a defense of inalienable human rights based strictly on the evolved cognitive capacities of well-functioning humans. But that defense is unconvincing, for various reasons that have been explained well in reviews of the book (for example, Jussi Suikkanen, 2016, "Robust Ethics," *Ethics* 126[2]: 541–545; and Angus Menuge, 2016, "Robust Ethics," *Faith and Philosophy* 33[2]: 249–253) and that I do not have the space or need here to unpack. Finally, even if his account succeeded, the human rights Wielenberg attempts to justify only pertain to those humans who are able to exercise certain evolved cognitive capacities—which not all living humans can exercise and which are highly variable in the extent of their exercise even among those who can—and thus does not qualify as a warrant for *universal* human rights.

Chapter 3

1. I am grateful to Steve Vaisey, Keith Meador, Todd Granger, Doug Porpora, Mike Wood, Justin Farrell, and Anna Sutherland for helpful feedback on an earlier version of this chapter.
2. See Andrews Abbott, 1988, *The System of Professions: An Essay on the Division of Expert Labor.* Chicago: University of Chicago Press.
3. New York: Harper.
4. Edward O. Wilson, 2014, *The Meaning of Human Existence.* New York: Liveright, p. 173; Wilson also writes: "there is no predestination, no unfathomable mystery of life. Demons and gods do not vie for our allegiance. Instead, we are self-made, independent, alone" (26).
5. Victor Stenger, "The Scientific Case against a God Who Created the Universe," in Michael Martin and Ricki Monnier (eds.), *The Improbability of God.* Amherst, NY: Prometheus, p. 28.
6. Richard Leakey and Roger Lewin, 1992, *Origins Reconsidered: In Search of What Makes Us Human.* New York: Doubleday, pp. 348–349.
7. Marcelo Gleiser, 2010, *A Tear at the Edge of Creation.* New York: Free Press, p. 226.

8. Reprinted in Russell, 1917, *Mysticism and Logic*. London: George Allen & Unwin, pp. 47–48.

9. Weinberg, 1993, New York: Basic Books, p. 154.

10. Quoted in Nancy Frankenberry, 2008, *The Faith of Scientists: In Their Own Words*. Princeton: Princeton University Press, p. 336.

11. Terry Eagleton, 2006, "Lunging, Flailing, Mispunching." *London Review of Books* 28(20) (October 19): 32–34.

12. Harari 109.

13. Weinberg, 2004, The Atheism Tapes, interview in 2003, audio series, episode 2.

14. Wilson 150, 154.

15. Linden, 2007, *The Accidental Mind: How Brain Evolution Has Given Us Love, Memory, Dreams, and God*. Cambridge, MA: Harvard University Press, pp. 232–233.

Chapter 4

1. Thanks to Atalia Omer, Slavica Jakelic, Heather Price, Phil Gorski, Meredith Whitnah, Dan Escher, Peter Mundey, Justin Farrell, and Katherine Sorrell for reading and commenting on a previous draft of this chapter, helping to improve it considerably. None of them is responsible for any errors or problems in the chapter. A different version of this chapter was previously published as Christian Smith, 2012, "Man the Religious Animal: We Are Naturally but Not Necessarily Religious," *First Things*, April.

2. Brad Gregory, 2012, *The Unintended Reformation: How a Religious Revolution Secularized Society*. Cambridge, MA: Harvard University Press.

3. James Byrne, 1997, *Religion and the Enlightenment*. Louisville: Westminster John Knox. This, of course, is the supposition of activist atheists today, exemplified most clearly by the leading New Atheists.

4. Rudolf Otto, 1958, *The Idea of the Holy*. New York: Oxford University Press; William James, 2009 [1902], *The Varieties of Religious Experience*. New York: Library of America; Mircea Eliade, 1987, *The Sacred and the Profane: The Nature of Religion*. New York: Harcourt Brace Jovanovich.

5. Russell McCutcheon, 2003, *Manufacturing Religion*. New York: Oxford; Tomoko Masuzawa, 2005, *The Invention of World Religions*. Chicago: University of Chicago Press; Talal Asad, 1993, *Genealogies of Religion*. Baltimore: Johns Hopkins University Press; Daniel Dubuisson, 2007, *The Western Construction of Religion*. Baltimore: Johns Hopkins University Press.

6. With regard to the latter thesis, I agree on these matters with Kevin Schilbrack, 2010, "Religions: Are There Any?," *Journal for the American Academy of Religion* 78(4) (November): 1112–1138, as well as with Martin Riesebrodt.

7. Andrew Greeley, 1972, *Unsecular Man*. New York: Dell; Bell, 1980, "The Return of the Sacred?," in *The Winding Passage*. New York: Basic Books; Rodney Stark and William Bainbridge, 1986, *The Future of Religion*. Berkeley: University of California Press; Rodney Stark and Roger Finke, 2000, *Acts of Faith*. Berkeley: University of California Press; Robert Bellah, 2011, *Religion in Human Evolution*. Cambridge, MA: Harvard University Press; Donald Miller and Tetsunao Yamamori, 2007, *Global Pentecostalism: The New Face of Christian Social Engagement*. Berkeley: University of California Press; Robert Bellah, 1967, "Civil Religion in America," *Daedalus* 96 (Winter): 1–21.

8. Steve Bruce, 2002, *God Is Dead*. New York: Blackwell; Bryan Wilson, 1979, *Contemporary Transformations of Religion*. Oxford, England: Oxford University Press; Pippa Norris and Ronald Inglehart, 2004, *Sacred and Secular*. Cambridge: Cambridge University Press; Phil Zuckerman, 2008, *Society without God: What the Least Religious Nations Can Tell Us about Contentment*. New York: New York University Press; Peter Berger, 1969, *The Sacred Canopy*. New York: Anchor Books. Also see David Voas and Mark Chaves, 2016, "Is the United States a Counterexample to the Secularization Thesis?," *American Journal of Sociology* 121(5): 1517–1556; Michael Hout and Claude Fischer, 2002, "Why More Americans Have No Religious Preference: Politics and Generations," *American Sociological Review* 67(2): 165–190.

9. Jose Casanova, 1994, *Public Religions in the Modern World*. Chicago: University of Chicago Press; Monica Toft, Daniel Philpott, and Timothy Shah, 2011, *God's Century: Resurgent Religion and Global Politics*. New York: Norton; Peter Berger (ed.), 1999, *The Desecularization of the World: Resurgent Religion and World Politics*. Grand Rapids, MI: Eerdmans.

10. See, for example, Paul Froese, 2008, *The Plot to Kill God: Findings from the Soviet Experiment in Secularization*. Berkeley: University of California Press; Fenggang Yang, 2011, *Religion in China: Survival and Revival under Communist Rule*. New York: Oxford University Press; Joseph Byrnes, 2005, *Catholic and French Forever: Religion and National Identity in Modern France*. State College: Pennsylvania State University Press. East Germany may be one exception, whose hypersecularity, David Martin notes, reflects "a bargain struck by its communist victors releasing its demoralized people from Nazi guilt if they accepted the complete secularist package." David Martin, 2011, *The Future of Christianity*. Farnham: Ashgate, p. 14.

11. Colin Renfrew and Iain Morley, 2009, *Becoming Human: Innovation in Prehistoric Material and Spiritual Culture*. Cambridge: Cambridge University Press.

12. Justin Farrell, 2015, *The Battle for Yellowstone: Morality and the Sacred Roots of Environmental Conflict*. Princeton: Princeton University Press; Robert Nelson, 2002, *Economics as Religion: From Samuelson to Chicago and Beyond*. State College: Pennsylvania State University Press; Thomas Dunlap, 2005, *Faith in Nature: Environmentalism as Religious Quest*. Seattle: University of Washington

Press; Robert Nelson, 2009, *The New Holy Wars: Economic Religion versus Environmental Religion in Contemporary America*. State College: Pennsylvania State University Press; Joseph Price, 2004, *From Season to Season: Sports as American Religion*. Macon, GA: Mercer University Press; William Cavanaugh, 2011, *Migrations of the Holy: God, State, and the Political Meaning of the Church*. Grand Rapids, MI: Eerdmans.

13. Lynn Schofield Clark, 2005, *From Angels to Aliens: Teenagers, the Media, and the Supernatural*. New York: Oxford University Press; Margaret Miles, 1997, *Seeing and Believing: Religion and Values in the Movies*. Boston: Beacon Press; Richard Bleiler, 2002, *Supernatural Fiction Writers: Contemporary Fantasy and Horror*. New York: Scribner's; Connie Neal, 2008, *The Gospel According to Harry Potter*. Louisville: Westminster John Knox.

14. Nancy Ammerman (ed.), 2007, *Everyday Religion: Observing Modern Religious Lives*. New York: Oxford University Press; Meredith McGuire, 2008, *Lived Religion: Faith and Practice in Everyday Life*. New York: Oxford University Press; Grace Davie, 2010, "Vicarious Religion," *Journal of Contemporary Religion* 25(2): 261–266; Grace Davie, 1994, *Religion in Britain since 1945*. Hoboken, NJ: Wiley-Blackwell. Also see Slavica Jakelić, 2010, *Collectivistic Religion: Religion, Choice, and Identity in Late Modernity*. Farnham: Ashgate. Furthermore, at least some traditional religions, including Christianity (per Saint Augustine, for example), have long argued that many apparently nonreligious activities—including drunken intoxication, wild carousing, promiscuous sex, harsh athletic training, committed political activism, incessant material consumption, drug addiction, and so on—represent deep human religious longings and searching and are actually misdirected quests for the true religious good. Such claims seem to tend to arise especially from traditions of monotheism and monism, both of which deny the possibility of the *ultimate* metaphysical existence of badness and evil.

15. But see Roy Bhaskar, 1998, *Critical Realism*. New York: Routledge; Andrew Collier, 1994, *Critical Realism*. London: Verso; Margaret Archer, 1995, *Realist Social Theory*. Cambridge: Cambridge University Press; Mats Ekström et al, 2002, *Explaining Society: Critical Realism in the Social Sciences*. New York: Routledge; Andrew Sayer, 2000, *Realism and Social Science*. New York: Sage; Roy Bhaskar, 1979, *The Possibility of Naturalism*. London: Routledge; Christian Smith, 2010, *What Is a Person?* Chicago: University of Chicago Press; Philip Gorski, 2009, "Social 'Mechanisms' and Comparative-Historical Sociology: A Critical Realist Proposal," in Björn Wittrock and Peter Hedström (eds.), *The Frontiers of Sociology*. Leiden: Brill, pp. 147–194.

16. Smith, 2017, *Religion: What It Is, How It Works, and Why It Matters*. Princeton: Princeton University Press, p. 22. Here I closely follow, though somewhat revise, the definition of religion advanced earlier by Martin Riesebrodt, who reformulated Melford Spiro's older definition. Martin Riesebrodt, 2010,

The Promise of Salvation: A Theory of Religion. Chicago: University of Chicago Press; also see Melford Spiro, 1966, "Religion: Problems of Definition and Explanation," in Michael Banton (ed.), *Anthropological Approaches to the Study of Religion*. London: Tavistock, pp. 87–126.

17. Riesebrodt defines religion as "a complex of practices that are based on the premise of the existence of superhuman powers, whether personal or impersonal, that are generally invisible." He writes: "The 'superhumanness' of these powers consists in the fact that influence or control over dimensions of individual or social human life and the natural environment is attributed to them—dimensions that are usually beyond direct human control. Religious practices normally consist in using culturally prescribed means to establish contact with these powers to gain access to them." Riesebrodt 74–75.

18. Smith, 2010. Chicago: University of Chicago Press.

19. Tom Tweed, 2017, *Heavenly Habitats: A History of Religion in the Lands That Became the United States*. New Haven: Yale University Press.

20. "Nonmaterial" meaning things like cultural beliefs, oral communications, shared values, etc. (not spirits, angels, etc., necessarily).

21. Smith, 2003, *Moral, Believing Animals: Human Personhood and Culture*. New York: Oxford University Press.

22. See, for example, Lynn Davidman, 1991, *Tradition in a Rootless World*. Berkeley: University of California Press.

23. Gregory 74.

24. Bell 333.

25. See Christian Smith (ed.), 2003, *The Secular Revolution*. Berkeley: University of California Press; Ann Taves, 2009, *Religious Experience Reconsidered*. Princeton: Princeton University Press; Phillip Gorski, 2000, "Historicizing the Secularization Debate," *American Sociological Review* 65(1) (February): 138–167.

26. Charles Taylor, 1992, *Sources of the Self*. Cambridge, MA: Harvard University Press.

27. One reader of the penultimate version of this chapter noted the lack of parallel in my argument that humans are inescapably moral animals but not inevitably religious creatures, given the close connections I have drawn between religion and morality. This in fact is my view. To be morally oriented and motivated is a condition impossible for human persons to escape (with the exception of psychopathological extremes, which none of us takes to be remotely normal or representative). Smith 2003; 2015, *To Flourish or Destruct: A Personalist Theory of Human Goods, Motivations, Failure, and Evil*. Chicago: University of Chicago Press. But, as I've observed here, humans can be, and many in fact are, not religious. Religion is a primary but not the only source of moral beliefs and commitments, so it is possible that moral orientation is a universal feature of human personhood while religious practice and belief are not.

28. Among persuasive works arguing this: Robert Kraynak, 2011, "Justice without Foundations," *New Atlantis*, Summer, 103–120; Alasdair MacIntyre, 1982, *After Virtue*. Notre Dame, IN: Notre Dame University Press.

29. Smith 2003.

30. William Cavanaugh, 2009, *The Myth of Religious Violence: Secular Ideology and the Roots of Modern Conflict*. New York: Oxford University Press.

31. Christian Smith and Brandon Vaidyanathan, 2010, "Religion and Multiple Modernities," in Chad Meister (ed.), *Oxford Handbook of Religious Diversity*. New York: Oxford University Press, pp. 250–265.

32. See Frank Pasquale and Barry Kosmin, 2013, "Atheism and the Secularization Thesis," in Stephen Bullivant and Michael Ruse (eds.), *The Oxford Handbook of Atheism*. New York: Oxford University Press, pp. 451–467.

Conclusion

1. See Brian Donohue, 2014, "God and Aristotelian Ethics," *Quaestiones Disputatae* 5(1): 65–77. Aristotle's argument for the existence of God as the Unmoved Mover is presented in book 12, chapters 6–10, of *Metaphysics* (New York: Penguin Classics, 1999).

2. The following are good starting points for exploring Aristotelian virtues ethics: Aristotle, 2003, *The Nicomachean Ethics*. New York: Penguin Classics; Michael Pakaluk, 2005, *Aristotle's Nicomachean Ethics: An Introduction*. Cambridge: Cambridge University Press; Richard Taylor, 2002, *Virtue Ethics: An Introduction*. Amherst, NY: Prometheus Books; Raymond Devettere, 2002, *Introduction to Virtue Ethics: Insights of the Ancient Greeks*. Washington, DC: Georgetown University Press; also see Alasdair MacIntyre, 1981, *After Virtue: A Study in Moral Theory*. Notre Dame, IN: University of Notre Dame Press; Christian Smith, 2010, *What Is a Person?: Rethinking Humanity, Social Life, and the Moral Good from the Person Up*. Chicago: University of Chicago Press, pp. 384–490.

3. For Aristotle, the reason the sensible knave turns out to be unhappy in life is not because he suffers grave psychological anxiety about his wrongdoing or the risk of being caught; nor because of violating the logical imperatives of rational reflection; nor because he fails to contribute to the maximization of humanity's utilitarian pleasures in relation to its pains. It is rather because reality is objectively ordered in such a way that sensible knavery compromises the exercise of the virtues necessary to realize a life of flourishing and happiness. It just won't happen. That is not a matter of autonomous individual choice. It is just the way reality is and works, which the sensible knave just cannot escape.

4. For an indirectly related discussion, see Christian Smith, 2014, *The Sacred Project of American Sociology*. New York: Oxford University Press.

INDEX